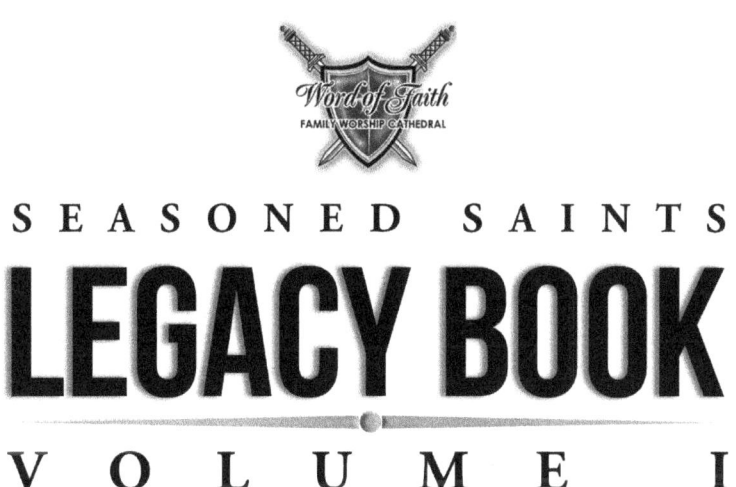

SEASONED SAINTS
LEGACY BOOK
VOLUME I

SEASONED SAINTS
LEGACY BOOK

INSPIRATIONAL STORIES OF FAITH, HOPE AND LOVE

Copyright ©2016 by Word of Faith Family Worship Cathedral, Seasoned Saints Ministry

All rights reserved. Except as permitted under the U.S. Copyright Act of 1076, no part of this publication may be reproduced, distributed or transmitted in any form or by any means, or stored in a database or retrieval system, without the prior written permission of the publisher.

Word of Faith Family Worship Cathedral
Seasoned Saints Ministry
212 Riverside Parkway
Austell, GA 30168

Visit our website at www.woffamily.org

Seasoned Saints Publishing is a ministry of
Word of Faith Family Worship Cathedral
The Word of Faith Family Worship Cathedral name and logo are trademarks
of Word of Faith Family Worship Cathedral

Cover and Layout Design by Mr. Merwin D. Loquias (whurn202@hotmail.com)

Printed in United States of America

First Volume: February 2016

ISBN: 978-0-9909142-0-4

This book is dedicated to Bishop Dale C. Bronner.
Your spiritual leadership equips us with the necessary tools
to live a life that God has purposed for each of us.
Your example inspires us to leave a legacy of greatness, charity and love.

"A disciple is not above his teacher, but everyone who is perfectly
trained will be like his teacher."

Luke 6:40

FOREWORD

BY BISHOP DALE C. BRONNER

The life that you live is the legacy that you leave! Everyone has a unique story of the fascinating journey of his/her life. The various nuances of our struggles and problems give interesting dynamics to our story. Personal stories are easier to relate to than just cold principles, and people love to hear good stories.

I want to commend the individuals who realize that God is writing an epic story with their life and who are bold enough to share it with others through this book. You see, legacy is not about the past; it is about what we set in motion for the future. For the Christian, our legacy includes our life message. Our life message has four components:

1.) Our testimony
2.) Our life lessons
3.) Our godly passions and
4.) The Good News (the message of salvation).

I've found that people are always more encouraged when we share how God's grace helped us in our weaknesses than when we brag about our strengths. Legacy is about what we share that blesses or impacts others. It draws upon the three distinct phases of life:

1.) Learning
2.) Earning
3.) Returning.

As you are enriched by the legacies of others, I want to encourage you to begin writing your story. Record the lessons that you learn in life, then share them with others. If you fail to record the lessons, the next generation will lose the blessing! So tell your story. Live your dream. Change your world!

LEGACY BOOK

CONTENTS

Legacy Legend *Rev. Emma Rowland* 14

A Fire Inside of Me *Monica Brown Allmond* 16

A Father-Daughter Date *George V. Amos, Jr.* 18

Use God's Word to Win *Dr. L.D. Anthony* 21

Always Trust God to Lead You *Shelley "Butch" Anthony, III* 23

His Will –Will Be Done *Mary Jolley Bailey, EdD* 25

Mama Lena *Lena Rebecca Wheat Barnes* 27

Relationships Are Everything *Claudia Barnett, PhD* 29

God Truly is a Healer *Constance Barnett* 32

Wisdom Speaks *Joyce Beeks* 33

My Life Remembered *Pansy Blevins* 35

There's Nothing Wrong With the Color of my Skin *Beth Bolden* 37

Surviving the Loss of Mother *Winifred Bonds* 39

Jesus Makes the Unbearable, Bearable *Elizabeth Boykin* 41

Finding Contentment in Every Situation *Kate Boykin* 42

Marriage Matters *Paul and Ingrid Cantrell* 44

Compromise But Don't Settle *Jacqueline Chapman* 45

Living My Vision *Shandra Childs-Thomas* 47

Love *Rev. Clarice W. Church* 49

The Turning Point *Dorothy Gibson Cobb* 50

A Legacy of Love *Mattie Copeland* 52

A Teacher's Story *Iris Davidson* 54

My Mother's Prayers *Rev. Edna Dillard* 56

Disadvantage is God's Advantage *Evangelist Carolyn Dixon* 58

Mama Knows Best *Alice Evans* 60

A Suitable Spouse *John Gibbons* 62

When You Least Expect It *Joyce. A. Gibbons* 64

Life Visions Realized *Betty A. Rice Gibson* 66

A Determined Life *Gloria A. Glass* 69

Christ in the Midst of a Crisis *Lillian Gray* 71

28 Days Later *Greg Green* 73

Pretty *Julia Copeland Green* 75

He Never Said He Was Sorry *Paula Palmer Green* 76

Don't Sweat the Small Stuff… Keep it Moving *Erika Zynette Greene* 79

Born Again *Evelyn Guinyard* 81

Faith Making Well *Joan Harvey Hadley* 83

Grandmother's Love Lingers *Joe Hadley, Jr.* 85

God's Plan of Compassion *Shirley Haile* 87

When My Feet Stopped Walking, My Heart Started Talking *Sher Harris* 89

The Teddy Bear Story *Rev. Carolyn Hanks Holley* 93

For a Giving…Not For a Living *Gilbert Hunter* 95

Missionary Nurse on a Mission *Shirley A. Hunter* 97

Do Not Allow Your Emotion to Run or Rule Your Life *Shirley L. Igberaese* 99

Green Means Go *A. Florence Gordon Jackson* 101

Set Apart for God's Purpose *Charles Johnson* 103

Why I Don't Hit Rock Bottom *Leanoria R. Johnson* 106

Keep Your Spiritual Vehicle Moving, Breaks Are Prohibited *Nathaniel Johnson* 108

The Significance of Mentorship *William Lee Johnson, Jr.* 110

Get Up, Pick Up and Pray Up *LaMonte E. Jones* 113

God Has a Path for You *Rudolph Jones* 115

Hard Work and Honesty Builds Character *Gladys Jordan* 117

Surrender to Win *Margot Jordan* 120

A Gift of Life and a Second Chance *Alice Marshall* 122

My Living Speaks *Fannie Moore May* 124

Use Me Lord *Margaret Wilson McCormick* 126

Ask God for the Answer *JoAnn McNear* 128

My Jesus, My Journey *Blanche Mills* 130

Things Change *Anita Ramsey Minniefield* 132

Power in Love *Curtis and Bobbie Minter* 134

Perception of Marriage *Leon and Angelia Noble* 136

How to Have a Happy Marriage *Robert and Joyce Norwood* 138

Serving Him with Hymns and Deeds *Ruth Schofield Parker* 140

Just Keep Having Birthdays *Mary Peeks* 142

Greatness Erupts *Preston Penn* 144

A Praying Woman of God *Selena Peoples* 147

Attitude Makes a Difference *Priscilla Wynn Peters* 149

Be Prepared, Be Ready, Be on Time *Lamar Reed* 151

Tied Up, Tangled Up and Turned Loose *Vera Reed* 152

Whatever You Do, Don't Lose Your Praise *Thelma Rig* 154

Graduation Dream Come True *Jacqueline Sims* 156

How I Met Myself *Greg Wayne Smith* 158

Power Twins of Trusting & Tithing *Teresa Charles-Smith* 161

The Instructions I Follow Determines the Future I Create *Thelma Talley* 163

Rain, Pain and Rainbows *Linda Taylor* 164

Not My Time *Patricia Terry* 167

In Life You Don't Need Easy, Just Possible *Ella Thompson* 170

A Ship Needs a Sail to Stay Afloat *Gwen Walker* 174

Let God Be God *Felisa Ward* 176

Till Death Do Us Part *Don Williams* 177

Television Fantasies Are Not Life's Reality *Nakita Williams* 179

The Shekinah Glory of God *Naomi Williams* 181

Down But Not Out *Paula Williams* *184*

Show Me You *Natarsha Wilson* *187*

Segregation in My Life: God's Directed Path *G. Patricia Woodward* *189*

Don't Judge a Book by Its Cover *Bernice G. Wright* *192*

Mama Always Came Through *Jackie D. Young* *194*

Message from Book Visionary and Project Manager *Paula Palmer Green* *197*

LEGACY LEGEND

REV. "MOTHER" EMMA ROWLAND, 99 YEARS YOUNG

**Mother Emma Rowland's
Ten Tips for Leaving a Legacy**

1. Remember to always put Jesus first – honor His commandments.
2. Teach what you know – make disciples.
3. Read your Bible daily for direction and always carry it with you to church.
4. Let God reveal your purpose.
5. Trust in God to show you what to do about all of your life situations.
6. Work hard and have a job even if you don't like it.
7. Pray, pray, pray for there is no future without God.
8. Surround yourself with young people.
9. Stay humble.
10. Embrace your spiritual gift and use it to glorify God.

Born to George and Malinda Walton in Omaha, Georgia, Mother Rowland is the seventh of nine siblings. At age 6, she experienced the death of her mother and was sent to be reared by her beloved grandmother. At age 7, by oil lamp, she became an avid reader. This was the start of her love for the Word of God. Early in life, she married Jim Pope. To that union they birthed two sons, Jim and Homer, and one daughter, Vera. She later wed G.P. Rowland and celebrated 32 years of blissful marriage until his passing. She was employed at Scripto Manufacturing Company and in 1978 she retired after 35 years of service. At age 37, Mother Rowland was called into the ministry. She was denied the opportunity to preach due to her gender. Knowing without a shadow of doubt her call was from God, she began to teach women. Today, she still teaches Sunday school. She became certified through the Institute of Biblical Studies under the leadership of Dr. Jerry Falwell and graduated with a degree in Bible Studies and Advanced Study Prophecies. On December 16, 2003, Bishop Dale C. Bronner ordained Mother Rowland as a minister of the Gospel for Word of Faith Family Worship Cathedral. When she is not studying the Word of God, she enjoys gardening, sewing, cooking and spending time with her grandchildren and great grandchildren. Though a world traveler, she is delighted to call Atlanta home.

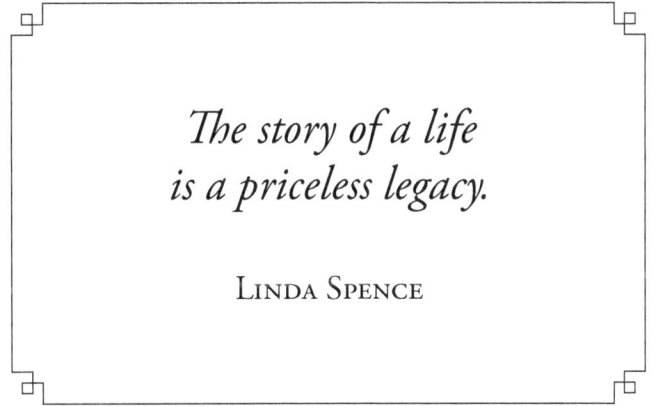

The story of a life is a priceless legacy.

LINDA SPENCE

A FIRE INSIDE OF ME

MONICA BROWN ALLMOND

My stepfather came into my life when I was in the seventh grade. I was living with my grandmother for a while, but then my life drastically changed when I moved in with my mother and stepfather. My stepfather was much older than my mother and was a provider of the basic needs for the family.

He was cold towards my sister and I, yet loving towards the daughter he and my mother birthed together. From middle to high school, my home life was miserable. I was often told, "You are going to have a house full of babies," and the young man I was seeing was going to destroy me. These tirades only made me angry and built a fire inside of me to show my stepfather that none of those things would come to pass. I was angry with my mother for not speaking on these episodes of negative prophecy. However, later in life I began to understand the helpless position she was in. He was the total provider for the household. He rescued her and her daughters and provided security. It was difficult for her to speak against someone who took care of all her needs.

As an escape, I spent a lot of time with my boyfriend and in the 11th grade, while on the honor roll, I became pregnant. During that time, getting pregnant while in high school was unacceptable. My stepfather told me I had to get married and get out of his house. I was devastated, frightened, lonely and confused. I had to withdraw from school because pregnant girls could not attend school with other students. A loving teacher informed me about the Crisis program, an educational program designed for pregnant students.

Not wanting to be an unwed mother, I got married and completed 11th grade in the Crisis program. My husband and I moved to a friend of my mother's house and rented a room upstairs. My husband joined the Army, so that we could have benefits and afford to take care of our child. He

went off to the service, and I had our son the summer after completing the 11th grade. The responsibility of being a young mother, living alone and trying to finish high school was quite a difficult task, but I was determined to finish high school.

I successfully graduated with my classmates and received my diploma. My son and I were blessed to be raised by a village. There were many women of wisdom that loved, supported and guided us. While I went to class, my best friend's mother kept my son. When I went to college my mother kept him during the week.

After completing high school, all my friends went to a local college, and their parents paid for their education. I desperately wanted to attend college too. I worked as a waitress at night to afford my bills and take care of my son. My son's father and I were no longer together, so I had to be the sole provider for our needs.

I was blessed to receive my bachelor's degree and moved to Atlanta to become a teacher. I quickly realized that my teaching salary would not pay all my bills. Without family or financial support, I continued to wait tables at night and teach during the day. It was difficult, but I was determined to provide a positive lifestyle for my son.

My son and I were blessed to beat the statistics. I finished high school, and he did too. According to statistics, a teenage mom and her child are likely to be high school dropouts. After completing high school, my son went into the Navy for one tour. He has been working in the restaurant industry since his return from the Navy. After his completion of high school, I returned to school to receive my master's degree.

I drove to West Georgia College twice a week after teaching. It was a grueling schedule, but I had a goal to complete. I taught school for over 20 years and during that time period, I counseled, motivated and supported many teen mothers. I shared my story to let them know they can accomplish their goals in life with determination. I encouraged them to use the negative things that were said or done to them to build a fire inside and prove the naysayers wrong.

In retrospect, I can see God's hand over my life. How did I complete high school on my own? How did I avoid the pitfalls of drugs, alcohol and a destructive lifestyle? I often ask myself these questions and realize that God sent people and situations into my life to assist me and keep me focused.

One of my favorite scriptures is Ephesians 3:20, "Now to Him who is able to do exceedingly abundantly above all that we ask or think, according to the power that works in us."

This scripture reminds me that God's plans for my life were so much greater than I imagined. When I think of my past when I was a frightened teen mother who wanted to complete high school and go to college so I could provide for my son, I see God had much bigger plans. I am so grateful for His love, divine guidance and protection.

The choices we make about the lives we live determine the kinds of legacies we leave.

TAVIS SMILEY

A FATHER-DAUGHTER DATE

GEORGE AMOS, JR.

When a father submits, he learns to commit. When he learns to commit, he learns to repent. Then, the order of the day is: submission, commitment then restoration.

Opportunities for negative, extracurricular activities were always available for young boys growing up in the hood of Southwest Chicago. At age 20, I searched for affirmation in an environment where having babies at an early age appeared to be normal and generational. A self-serving behavior ruled my choices even while being raised with eight other siblings by both parents. My parents have been married over 50 years and still live in the same house where I was raised. They often talked to me and my siblings about the consequences of sex and pregnancy.

I began dating a young lady who decided she was going to remain a virgin until marriage. I thought, "Wow, that's great, she will remain faithful to me while I continue my quest to seek and conquer." She dated me faithfully for over a year. I made my rounds around town with other girls whilst increasing the pressure on my girlfriend to give in to my sexual demands. After finally succumbing to the pressure of my full-court press in November 1982, my oldest daughter was born out of wedlock. My girlfriend, a 17-year-old mother, was filled with hopes of a future with me, a 20-year-old boy with no plan or vision for the future. I was uncommitted to the Lordship of Jesus Christ.

I spent five years running in place with no vision, no plan and a five year-old daughter who was growing daily. Change seemed impossible. My future wasn't bright, and I saw no light at the end of the tunnel. The possibility of my daughter having married parents was slim. Basically, my daughter's dreams were shattered. She was added to the casualties of my past, a past that covered me with a tremendous amount of guilt and anger.

Through it all, I knew life had something more to offer than the road I was traveling. So, I began my journey out of state. Something inside of me said, "There's more to life." In 1987, I said goodbye to Chicago and hello to Atlanta. Finally, I felt free to dream and live with a purpose in a place where I could start over. Little did I know, I could change the place but the people and the self-serving behavior of the past would come along. Once I settled in Atlanta with a job and residence, I became a seasonal dad. I visited my daughter in Chicago during the summer breaks and occasionally on the weekends. I bought my daughter nice things to assure her of my love.

Fast forward eight years. In 1994, I met the love of my life, and we married. A year later, my life changed. I encountered the true and living God, Jesus Christ. I went from serving myself to serving others. The fellowship of others began to speak guidance towards my family. My wife gave birth to my second daughter in 1996. Shortly after, my oldest daughter who at the time was 15 years old, moved into our home. Two years later, we gave birth to our son. Now, the responsibility of marriage and family went to another level.

The changes in my life caused me to learn how to submit. When I say submit, I mean submit to the Lordship of Jesus Christ and allow Him to be my guide. Despite life's twists and turns, I stayed on the right track. I had a vision, purpose and plan.

However, as life would have it, my oldest daughter began to display resentment and bitterness. She had a problem seeing me as a loving and committed father that she didn't have. It was something she missed and longed for. In turn, this caused tension in my home. Eventually, she graduated high school and enrolled into the U.S. Navy.

Several years passed and the relationship between my daughter and I hadn't improved much. Our contact was like two ships passing in the night. On many occasions, our conversations were brief. Because of the lack of strength in our relationship, we both felt pain. We were full of pride and stubborn. We settled in our minds that our relationship had no chance of reconciliation.

Regardless of the situation, a father should repent for what he's done wrong. As a father you may feel that you've done everything correctly and you are justified in your actions of sometimes holding your children to the wall. Your actions may prompt you to ask yourself, "Is being right better than being alone?" That is a tough question to grapple with. After all is said and done, God gave it all up for us. On the cross, He said, "Forgive them for they don't know what they have done." I decided my relationship with my daughter was far more valuable than hurt feelings or acts of disrespect.

During my weekly prayer time with my prayer accountability partner, God revealed to me that I had the keys to reconcile my relationship with my daughter. I'd just about given up hope. But God said, "You repent, make the first move and I will do the rest." One Monday morning God said, "Text her now!" I'm reasoning with God like, "Why? She's not going to call me back, and if she does what am I going to say?" He said, "Just do it."

Well, I stepped out on a limb. At this point, my daughter was no longer speaking to me. She was not accepting or returning my phone calls and text messages. So, I thought, "Okay, here goes nothing." My text read, "Hey please give me a call. I'm no longer interested in bickering with you." Ten minutes later my phone rang and it was her! When a father repents, reconciliation is sure to follow.

I said to my daughter, "I'm sorry I left you at five years old. At that time in my life I wasn't fit to be a father. But, it's no excuse for leaving you. I'm sorry, and I love you very much. Can we make a fresh start?" She replied, "Yes," as we both drowned in tears.

We enjoyed breakfast together on the following Saturday morning. I decided that this would be one serious date. I showered and put on fresh clothing and cologne. We met for breakfast and embraced each other with a huge hug.

I explained to my daughter, "I feel like I'm on a date with a girl I've always wanted to date, but she never accepted." She finally accepted. I dressed and cleaned up nicely, because this day was very special. This was a date I always wanted.

Romans 8:18 says, "For I consider that the sufferings of this present time are not worthy to be compared with the glory which shall be revealed in us."

I'm no longer on the fence of who I am. I am fully committed to my wife, children and family. I have learned when a father submits, he commits. He commits at all costs regardless of what obstacles he has to face. I am no longer a runner; I am rooted firmly.

There came a time when the risk to remain tight in the bud was more painful than the risk it took to blossom.

ANAIS NIN

USE GOD'S WORD TO PREVAIL THRU BATTLE TO WIN THE WAR

DR. L.D. ANTHONY

Dr. Linette de Loatch Anthony

What would I tell my younger self or future generations? When in conflict situations, do not allow your feelings and emotions to rule! One must use God's Word to bring wisdom to your head and compassion to your heart! This approach will allow you to be discerning in a battle to win the war!

Why is this truth/ritual significant to me? You can be successful at applying God's Word to renew your mind and change your approach in most conflicts to elicit a good and successful outcome. To do this, one needs to learn an encouraging scripture and apply it daily. Read the Word with passion and purpose. Immerse yourself in it wholeheartedly. Pray using sustaining scriptures so they become mantras (chants in your head) by repeating them and allowing them to seep into your soul. Write them upon the table of your heart so you can apply them instantly. Believe God at His Word! When confronted, apply and engage God's Word in the situation to allow the outcome to be less contentious.

Who, when, where and how I came to know this? I think back on a life changing situation from years ago. One evening, I was home preparing a wonderful dinner for my family. The kids and I were home, but my husband was very late coming home. So, the kids and I went ahead and ate without him. Long after 9 p.m., my husband came in unapologetically as if it was 5 p.m., which was his normal arrival time. This was unlike him. Usually, he would call or warn me in the morning if he was coming home late. In this particular situation, he didn't give me a heads up or call. I was upset about him missing dinner with us, but I was more upset about how worried I was. I thought something bad happened. We did not have cell phones like we do today. Without any communication from him, I was left to think something bad happened as the evening hours passed.

Needless to say, when he finally came in the door, I was livid and did all I could to pretend I wasn't upset. I asked calmly, "Where have you been and why didn't you call?" Even though I was angry, I reached to give him an emotionless kiss while questioning him again, "Why are you so late coming home?" His reply was not what I expected; he was almost five hours late. He replied, "I decided to stop and have drinks with the fellas after work." At this point I couldn't even look or speak to him. Next, I inquired if he ate and he replied, "No." So, I warmed his food and fixed his plate. He sat down and started eating like he was eating the "Last Supper." He ate so aggressively that he never looked up. After seeing how he was devouring the food and didn't even care enough to call and let me know he was going to be late, I became enraged!

Instead of concentrating on an encouraging scripture, the demonic stronghold of anger took control of me. I grabbed his plate of food and threw it in the kitchen sink and yelled, "Next time you need to eat where you are or care enough to call your family!" He jumped up and asked, "What is wrong with you? Why would you throw my food away while I am eating it?" At that point, the encounter became a full-blown fight.

Now that I have a stronger relationship with God, I replay this incident in my mind. That night would have turned out differently if I allowed myself to get into the spirit by using positive scripture reinforcement. Instead, my actions became carnal or fleshly. In the spirit, I wouldn't have allowed my hurt feelings and my racing emotions to control my actions and take over my heart with anger.

If I had known what I know now, that night would have ended so differently. I would have implemented God's Word in my heart and mind instead of allowing such demonic force to take control. I would've used my spiritual weapon, God's Word, the "Sword of the Spirit" to express my feelings and emotions. Instead, they ran wild. When my husband finally arrived home, I would've managed my emotions and anger. As soon as I felt them changing for the worse, I would've taken control of them through the spirit. This would have allowed enough time for my emotions to settle and have a meaningful conversation to address the issue with calmness and concern.

As one author, Robert Quillen, once wrote, "A happy marriage or relationship is the union of two good forgivers." Forgiveness was never considered during this encounter – only wrath. Now that I have grown spiritually, given that same situation, I would have silently chanted scriptures, Psalms 145:8, "The LORD is gracious, and full of compassion; slow to anger, and of great mercy; or Ecclesiastes 7:9, "Be not hasty in your spirit to be angry: for anger rests in the bosom of fools."

By doing this, I would have felt the scripture's calming effect. Dwelling on and repeating the scripture like a mantra would have allowed God's spirit to take over my fleshy actions and thoughts.

> *"Everyone should be quick to listen, slow to speak and slow to become angry, because human anger does not produce the righteousness that God desires."*
>
> JAMES 1:19-20

ALWAYS TRUST GOD TO LEAD YOU

SHELLEY "BUTCH" ANTHONY III

Being able to serve the Lord wholeheartedly in a regular place of worship is important to me. As my walk with God grew stronger, there came a time and a need for me and my family to seek the next level in God, particularly after being a part of one ministry for over 25 years. God was creating a major shift in our spiritual journey. I knew my family and I needed to be under the covering and teaching of one who would pour into our spirits profoundly. Thanks be to God; He led us to Word of Faith Family Worship Cathedral. I shall forever be grateful for the confirmation God granted me which let me know that our steps had been ordered by God to be a part of the Word of Faith family.

As of this year, I am a student of Bishop Bronner, and I have listened to his powerful teachings of God's Word for more than four years. Because this was a fairly new process to me, I wasn't really sure how to begin. Granted, before we joined Word of Faith, I served in ministry as a deacon then as an elder and an associate pastor. Nevertheless, I still wondered where my spiritual journey would take me. How could I continue to provide my family with spiritual guidance in a totally new environment?

After much prayer and many conversations with my wife, Diane, God showed me that Word of Faith would be the next level that my family and I were so earnestly seeking. It is amazing how God will smile on you and give you confirmation on certain things. The timing of when He gives the confirmation is amazing as well. You see, He may not give you the confirmation early on; it could take years. This is what happened to me even though I knew in my heart that Word of Faith was the place for my family and me.

After a recent conversation with Pastor Hobbs, one of the pastors in the ministry, he said he wanted me to meet Pastor Whitely, who is over the Discipleship Group Ministry. He also told me, "It's your time." Some time passed by, and I traveled to Orlando to check on a project. As I was there, I was afforded the opportunity to meet with a young man who was a fellow believer. As we talked, I told him about myself being a part of the Word of Faith family and how much I appreciated the leadership and teachings of Bishop Bronner. As we continued our dialogue, he shared with me the frustrations he was experiencing in his teaching ministry. It was to the point where he was seriously considering bowing out of it altogether. The conversation continued and he recalled Bishop Bronner delivering a very dynamic message at his church a while back. He also told me he was the driver that picked Bishop Bronner up from the airport when he came to Orlando. It's a small world after all.

This brother and I continued to talk about the goodness of Jesus. As we were doing so, the Holy Ghost took over. We ministered to each other tremendously. After almost two hours, he decided to go back to his teaching ministry. He knew that God had sent me to finish up where Bishop Bronner left off. What an awesome experience that was! It proved to be confirmation of where I am supposed to be and how it is meant for me to serve Bishop Bronner, Dr. Nina Bronner and God's people.

Sometimes life can cause you to second guess, especially if you find yourself in a place you never thought you would be. I never dreamed my family and I would be looking for the next level in a church home, especially after so many years and memories. And even though it happened, I'm so grateful to know God will never leave His children alone. Proverbs 3:5-6 instructs us to trust in the Lord with our whole heart. We are not to lean to our own understanding; rather, we should acknowledge Him in all our ways, and He shall direct our paths. I thank the Lord for allowing me to trust Him!

> *But as for me and my household, we will serve the Lord.*
>
> JOSHUA 24:15

HIS WILL – WILL BE DONE

MARY JOLLEY BAILEY, EdD

There is a familiar saying, "If you want to make God laugh, tell Him your plans." As a teenager and young adult, I had all my life's work planned and knew without a doubt the direction it was going to take in regards to my career. My story is about the importance of coming to the realization that God's plan is superior to any we could ever imagine. I will tell you how I came to trust in God's will and some of the major events that followed.

As the only child, I spent many hours entertaining myself and rather enjoyed it. As a little girl, I set up an office and I was the bookkeeper, stenographer and file clerk. The office was not elaborate and contained no furniture. It was only a small area in our living room where I performed these imaginary assigned tasks. These play activities turned into a dream I carried into my high school years. I was definitely going to attend a business school after graduating high school and become a secretary, or so I thought. During my junior year in high school, certain students were invited to meet with the Dean of Students from Clark College in Atlanta, Georgia. I went with no intention of going to college, but I decided to join the other students in hearing what the dean had to say. When I left that room, my entire outlook on life after high school changed. Dean Hamilton spoke with such conviction and warmth about Clark College; I felt obligated to go there. I believed he would surely look after me if I attended, and there was obviously no other institution to consider. That morning spent with Dean Hamilton in the library at Washington High School changed my life, and I am sure it was divine intervention.

After my graduation from Clark with a business degree and a minor in education, I applied to teach but obviously God had other plans. I was unable to find a job in business education at the high schools in Atlanta. The schools were segregated, and there were very few teaching positions in that field. Instead, I was hired with the U.S. Department

of the Army as a secretary and remained in federal service for a few years. After about seven years, I still wanted to teach. So I prepared myself for entry into the field of elementary education. As a very competitive person, I didn't like being at the entry level of any profession when all of my old college classmates were far ahead of me. I was constantly seeking positions to apply for.

One morning as I was praying to God for direction, I finally said with sincerity, "Let Your will, not mine, be done." This was very difficult for me. I thought I precisely knew the job I wanted to strive for in the school system. However, I wasn't sure if it was the job God wanted me to have. I wanted the answer to my prayers to be what I wanted. Surprisingly, the decision to allow God to be the decision maker in my career hunt would elicit a major turning point in my life. Once I kept my prayers consistent, my career took a drastic turn. Even though I was oblivious as to what was happening, I was surrounded by people who would shape my career in ways I never imagined. My experience and education prepared me for the next door God opened.

During the years following my decision to earnestly and sincerely ask for God's will, I began to teach my two girls the importance of making this prayer commitment. My youngest daughter began to pray for a mate and made a decision to wait on God's guidance and intervention in all her relationships. Praying for His will in her life (rather than moving on without His guidance) has resulted in a very happy marriage with her soul mate.

The last position I held prior to retirement was as an Executive Director with the responsibility of managing a department that oversaw the expenditure of federal funds. Some of the responsibilities required knowledge of the skills I dreamed about as a child. I believe God planted the seed in my mind as a child to begin to prepare me for the career in my future. God's plans for my life were on a much higher level than imagined. As a high school student, I could not even dream of earning several degrees and having the positions and titles I've earned. Throughout my career and life, I've continued to close my prayers with, "Let Your will, not mine, be done." I have learned that if we trust in God, we will experience joys and achievements far greater than we could ever dream or imagine. To God be the glory.

> *For I know the plans I have for you, declares the Lord, plans to prosper you and not to harm you, plans give you hope and a future.*
>
> ~ JEREMIAH 29:11

MAMA LENA

LENA REBECCA WHEAT BARNES

Mama Lena was born December 11, 1928. She is the oldest of four daughters to the late John Wesley and Rebecca Wheat, fondly known as Daddy Johnny and Mama Becky. Her mother had ten children – four girls and six boys. John and Rebecca raised their children to always trust in God.

At the age of 8, Lena learned to cook for her family. Her father built her a foot stool so she could reach the stove. Her father was a hard worker and a minister. He and Rebecca were believers in the gospel and strong prayer warriors.

John worked for Bell Aircraft, now known as Lockheed, and Pepsi Cola Company as a janitor. Daddy Johnny and Mama Becky invited several different families into their home when fathers were absent or lost their jobs.

Despite her father always being employed, and sometimes even at two jobs, Lena remembers Christmases when she and her siblings only received one apple and one orange each. With ten children, times could be quite hard. One Christmas, they only received half of an apple and an orange. Lena and her sister Elizabeth, who is next in age, recall when they used to go outside and play in the grass. They would plait the grass and pretend it was their doll's hair. They called their dolls Ms. Frokes and Ms. Frisee (Fry-see). Lena says these were the "good ol' days." Her past experiences helped shape and mold her life to who she is today.

Lena developed a strong work ethic and has worked all of her life to care for her children. She is a feisty 86-year-old and still works a half day on most Fridays. She birthed nine children, four girls and five boys, whom she mostly raised alone. Two of her sons are now deceased. In 1967 when her sister Elizabeth was in an almost-fatal accident, Lena cared for Elizabeth's four children for a year in addition to caring for her own nine children.

Lena is a woman of prayer and loves the Lord. She is a blessed woman of God. Lena said that, "I pray that all of my children will be well and will turn to the Lord." She tried to raise them the best she could and always taught them to fear and reverence the Lord.

At age 71, Lena married for a second time to Francis Barnes whom she loved deeply. She cared for her ill husband until he passed in August 2014.

Lena is a wonderful cook. Fortunately, her children and grandchildren inherited this trait. Her claim to fame is her Sour Cream Pound Cake. Her favorite sayings are, "Lord have Mercy" and "The Lord takes care of His own."

Mama Lena's Sour Cream Pound Cake

1 Box Duncan Hines Butter Recipe Pound Cake Mix
2 eggs
1 cup of sour cream
½ cup of vegetable oil
Mix and pour in greased/floured pan
Bake for 45 minutes at 350

RELATIONSHIPS ARE EVERYTHING

CLAUDIA BARNETT, PhD
AKA DR. KLAW

We are born into a world that has predetermined our initial relationship. Just to think, I am here based on the fact that my parents were in relationship and so are you, no matter how brief.

As we grow, we have the ability to determine the type and quality of the relationships that we desire. That is also true of our spiritual life. Salvation is built on the foundational relationship with Jesus Christ. Our choice is to choose Him as our Lord and Savior. Once we desire to know Him better, all of our other relationships will be influenced.

I grew up in Harlem, New York, for the first six years of my life. The hustle and bustle of New York City streets were the everyday sounds of life. I lived across the street from a fire station which signified the pains of everyday life; a loss was occurring, or someone was in trouble. Although I was born in that environment, I did not feel comfortable. As I was told in the past, I was a displaced New Yorker. I am the last of three children born to my parents. I am known as "The baby." Every family seems to have one.

At age 7, my parents moved to Northeast Bronx and purchased a home. I lived in a mixed environment consisting of Italians, Jews and Blacks. We all lived on the same street, also known as "the block." Similar to our neighbors, my parents were immigrants as well. My father is from Kingston, Jamaica, and my mother is from Port Limon, Costa Rica. My mother's family migrated to Jamaica for a better life; her father went there to do farm work. You see, New York City was a melting pot in the 60s, and everyone worked well together.

Throughout grade school, I attended a public school in Co-Op City (formerly known as Freedom Land, a type of amusement park). I graduated from Harry S. Truman High School and was proud to be one of the first few classes to graduate. My class was full of "Mustang Pride." Most of us didn't live in Co-Op City, so it was an honor to be chosen to

attend Harry S. Truman due to our high academic standings.

High school represented a time in which our life paths were established – if we paid attention. We were in relationships with people from our classes, our bus stops and those we walked home with. We laughed, joked and cried together, but, we didn't fully understand the dynamics of relationships.

Some of my classmates went on to college far away while some of us remained local. Honestly, college was not on the agenda for everyone. Establishing a vocation in which we could be self-sufficient and eventually take care of our families was the main focus. For guys, learning a trade was important and for girls, learning secretarial skills was important. These were trades and skills that we could always fall back on to make ends meet. Typing and cooking classes were open to anyone, and childcare was also available. As teenagers, we wanted to get out of high school so we could "live our life" like recording artist Junior sang. As our final years approached in high school, we knew we had decisions to make. I didn't plan to attend college, primarily because I had older siblings who were currently enrolled in college but didn't seem to have progressed much in life. I wanted to see a major change for those who were investing all of their time into school. Little did I know, they were gaining knowledge they didn't share with me! In retrospect, we didn't receive much guidance regarding our academic future. We were not encouraged to go outside of our surroundings, as it was such a big world out there. As a result, I never applied for colleges during my senior year in high school. However, I earned nine college credits during my junior year from taking after-school classes offered by the local four year university.

I wanted to do something productive with my life, so I asked my close friend what was she planning to do after graduation. She shared that she was going to study communications and work in the entertainment industry. I was impressed that she knew exactly what she wanted. She was aligning herself to actively pursue her goal. She told me about the program she successfully completed during high school. The program allowed her to gain practical experience. She shared with me the details, and I asked questions to see how I could take advantage of the same opportunity.

During my last year in high school, I was exposed to the Executive High School Internship Program. I knew I wanted to work with people and I knew I was intrigued with peoples' thoughts. I had no idea the name for this was psychology. This was a big word that was tossed around on TV by intellectuals. Because of my eagerness to help people, I was placed in an Outpatient Alcoholic Treatment Center in a local hospital. I worked directly with a psychiatrist. I was able to experience group and one-on-one therapy sessions.

Because I did not prepare to go to college, I was forced to work. I saved money to afford at least one semester of college. I worked in the spring and summer and enrolled for the fall semester. I was excited about receiving training and an education that would prepare me for my passion.

College was interesting as I developed life-long relationships there. Trying to find my way, I was involved with various clubs and organizations. I insisted that my voice to be heard. At one point I became president of a club, and I spoke up for my peers and colleagues. In my junior year of college, my professor asked me if I was interested in becoming a student representative on the College Curriculum Committee. Because of my relationship with this particular professor, I accepted the opportunity. She was a prime example of a successful female professor. I enjoyed our student-professor relationship, and her life spoke volume to me. I graduated college knowing that I was there to make a difference. The relationships I gained along the way were a part of God's plans for my life.

Shortly after marriage, I moved to New Jersey. I became a mother, and I began realizing how quickly my life was changing. I was no longer a student or even a recent college graduate; I was a mom now. I was thankful that I still had strong relationships with the individuals I grew up with inside and outside of the church. My church sisters and brothers established spiritual accountability as neighborhood friends and colleagues.

In spring of 1987, I decided to go back to school to earn my master's degree. I strongly desired to continue my education. I discussed this decision with my parents. Despite my father's terminal illness, he encouraged me to pursue my desires. I heeded his advice and completed the enrollment application a week later. A month later, my father passed. My relationship with my dad was special. He always gave me great and wise counsel.

I relocated to Georgia after graduate school. My biological and church families were no longer around the corner or even the next state over. They were 900 miles away. Although this was a big move, it was one that I was yearning for. I wanted to expand my horizons.

I moved to Atlanta in 1990. This was before Atlanta won the bid to host the '96 Olympics. Things were looking up for the South. I thought, "Perhaps, I made the right move." Atlanta grew by leaps and bounds. Once the Olympics came, it was different. Traffic became unavoidable. Packing a lunch to go visit someone locally was the norm!

My family grew, and there were two additions to the family – three children in all. Because of the large age difference between my children, I felt like each child was the "only" child. My life was centered on ensuring that my children had the necessary foundation to be successful.

In the fall of 2006, I decided to go back to school to start a doctoral program. I did not mention this before, but I was accepted to a B.A. to Ph.D. program before I completed undergraduate school. I was also accepted again in the spring of 2003, but I made the decision not to go based on my relationship at the time. Twenty-five years later, I started a program that encompassed my professional aspiration. It was all on God's time. In comparison with past relationships, I realized my relationship with the Lord has been the most consistent throughout life. Although a significant amount of time passed, God promised certain things to me that His Word confirmed. Delay does not mean denial; everything happens in His appointed time.

I asked the Lord to restore me to the years that was "eaten by the cankerworm." And He did! I was able to complete a seven-year B.A. to Ph.D. program in less than three years! I am living my purpose by aiding future Ph.D. and doctoral students through the dissertation process. I am a doctoral mentor who has aided over 200 doctors through the process of becoming a scholar practitioner.

Relationships are important, and it is my desire to make sure those in my life understands that.

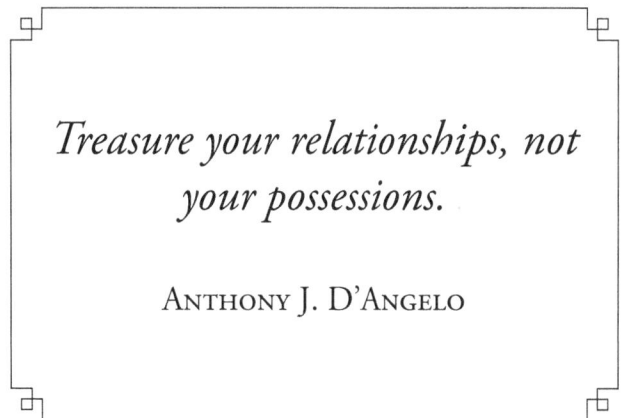

Treasure your relationships, not your possessions.

ANTHONY J. D'ANGELO

HOW I LEARNED THAT GOD IS A HEALER

CONSTANCE BARNETT

Constance E. Barnett

Uttering, "I have breast cancer," was the beginning of my healing journey.

I lost my mom to stomach cancer in 2007. A year later, I was diagnosed with breast cancer. This moment felt like a blow to my stomach.

"How could this happen to me?" "Why did this happen to me?"

As my doctor shared my diagnosis over the phone, I was so calm that it was scary. As he explained what our next steps would be, I tried to process all of the information. It felt so unreal. The first person I called to share the news was my baby sister. I began to cry, but God did not allow me to wallow in my sadness for long before He began to strengthen me in spirit. God put "unction" in me to learn everything I could about breast cancer, and He promised to do the rest. I immediately went home and started my research. God put the right people in my path, surrounded me with praying saints, family and friends and even allowed me to form new friendships with individuals who were or once were cancer patients.

Throughout my treatments, God was present in spirit. During chemotherapy, each session was expected to get a little harder but not in my case. God did the total opposite! My doctors and I were amazed at how God took me through the chemo and radiation treatment almost unscathed; just like the three men in the Bible, Shadrach, Meshach, and Abednego, who went into the burning furnace but came out untouched.

God is truly my healer, because I've had a first-hand experience that no one can ever take away from me. I am in my sixth year of being cancer free!

> *Then they cried out to the Lord in their trouble, And He saved them out of their distresses. "He sent His word and healed them, And delivered them from their destructions. Oh, that men would give thanks to the LORD for His goodness, And for His wonderful works to the children of men!*
>
> PSALM 107:19-21

WISDOM SPEAKS

JOYCE BEEKS

By worldly standards, my mother was extremely beautiful. She was a sweet, kind, gentle and encouraging woman. She never bothered or said anything negative about anyone. My mother would often say, "My actions only hurt myself." As the eldest of six children, all born out of wedlock, I found her statement to be false. I felt lonely, alone and insecure. Her actions did not hurt herself only.

Each time I filled out a form requiring information about my father, I was embarrassed. Not only was my last name different from his, my mother would not allow me to list his name at all. I could not tell anyone who my father was, because it would bring shame to his family, although his family knew who I was. I learned to be secretive versus transparent. As I mentioned before, my mother's actions did not hurt her only.

School was challenging for me, but I made good grades. From fifth through ninth grade, one specific child at school taunted me by saying things like, "Who is your father?", "Your mother is having another bastard," "You think you are cute." She would also talk about me to other children.

My mother's income did not afford us the opportunity to live in the better parts of the city, but all students of color attended the same high school. Since elementary school, I knew that I wanted to become a registered nurse (RN). Attending career days at school taught me about classes I needed to take and possible schools I could attend to reach my goal. Despite the lack of interest or guidance from the school counselors and teachers, I tried to pursue my educational goals on my own.

As a child, I knew about God because I attended church regularly. However, I never felt like I could be faithful to Christ. I didn't understand that once

I accepted Christ, I would be empowered to live a Christian life. Later in life after accepting Jesus Christ as my Savior and the Lord of my life, I began to read the Bible and become enlightened. I became aware of my identity in Christ, forgave those who hurt me and made myself available to be used by Him.

After completing nursing school, God sent me a husband and two lovely children. I continued my education, received higher degrees and additional certifications in nursing. When I went back to high school class reunions, I would go over to greet my high school teachers and show my respect. On one occasion, a teacher shared with me that my former homeroom teacher had not expected me to succeed in life. Also, at a class reunion, fellow classmates from my side of town shared information that I wasn't aware of; the teachers in high school did not think we would succeed, and that is why they did not provide college or career counseling.

A truly successful life is one in which you have an intimate relationship with Jesus Christ. He provides everything we need to live in victory; walk in it!

Lessons learned:

1. Everyone sins, even parents and teachers.
2. You never only hurt yourself when you sin.
3. When you ask God for forgiveness of your sins and accept Jesus' death and resurrection as payment for your sins, God does not condemn you, He forgives you.
4. God loves, cares, leads and guides you even before you accept Christ into your life.
5. God had a plan for me, and He has a plan for your life. Find out His plan for your life.
6. God is using me to tell others about Him, and He can use you if you let Him.

> *"And not only that, but we also glory in tribulations, knowing that tribulation produces perseverance; and perseverance, character; and character, hope. Now hope does not disappoint, because the love of God has been poured out in our hearts by the Holy Spirit who was given to us.*
>
> ROMANS 5:3-5

LIFE LEGACY TO REMEMBER

PANSY BLEVINS

When I was a young lady I lived on my own terms. I always felt I was different. Some called me wild, crazy and unpredictable, but I called myself a child of God. Once I began to embrace my flaws and realize that they hold a great responsibility, that's when I began to live a shameless life. As I got older, I began to face many trials and tribulations, but I learned quickly that prayer is the answer to all things. There is nothing that we go through where God is not with us; He is there to bring us out. Nothing on earth can take my God from me. I have Jesus inside of me!

I remember struggling trying to get my business started. There were two days left to submit a mountain of paperwork. I prayed and reminded myself that God did not bring me this far to leave me. I eventually gathered all of the necessary paper work and faxed it to the appropriate office. I was so pleased to learn that my application was approved. Within three days, I received my business license. The process was tedious since this was my first experience. Unfortunately, I didn't have anyone to walk me through the process. This is an example of how God is in control no matter how many odds are against you. I am a strong believer in prayer and maintaining a close relationship with God.

I know my path has been ordered by the Lord. I believe that every person you come in contact with has a special purpose in your life. I met my husband when I was heading home after a trip to the grocery store. The weather was harsh; it was snowing that evening. My car wasn't working

properly, so I caught the train home. Once I arrived near my house, I walked home carrying a handful of bags. Upon approaching my house, a handsome man greeted me. He asked if he could help me carry my grocery bags. I declined. He was persistent and continued to ask, but I still replied, "No, thank you. I'm ok."

It was something about the final time he asked that made me give in. We talked while he carried my bags. Once we got to my doorstep he asked if he could come and visit me. I immediately declined, but his persistence paid off. Eventually I agreed to him coming over. The next day he came by and we sat and stared at each other. It was then that I knew he was a gift from God and the man for me. Today, we have been together for 28 years! It has not been easy, but it is all worth it. I thank God for giving me my other half and for all of the special people He has placed in my life.

I talk to my grandson, Makario, often about praying and keeping God first in his heart and mind. Makario is only 9 years old. Nevertheless, I believe in the Word, and God instructs us in Proverbs 22:6 to, "Train up a child in the way that he should go, and when he is old he will not depart from it." I am not perfect, but I make it my daily mission to follow God's Word and be a disciple. I love Gospel music and attending church. When I miss a weekly service, I notice that my day isn't prosperous. But I ask God to help me by saying, "This is the day You have made for me to be joyful and happy. I ask for my sins to be forgiven." I live my life to serve God and others. I enjoy helping people buy food and clothes. I also enjoy helping people in hospitals and nursing homes. I know God will never leave me and I have favor over my life. Because I have favor, I make it my mission to be a blessing to others.

I look back over my life and see where God has brought me from. During my struggles and challenging times, I knew I had to depend upon God for His safety and peace. My faith in the Lord endures even in the worst situations. God acts on behalf of those who wait on Him and trust and believe in His Word. At times the suffering you go through will seem immensely unfair, especially when it occurs at the hand of another person, but you have to believe that the most powerful thing you can do is pray. God is greater than any problem. We must trust God with whatever we face. I count my blessings and look for opportunities to shine. The most important thing I can do is connect with God by reading His Word and spending time in prayer. This method has given me direction, strength and focus. I fight all my battles on my knees; prayer is my life. The Lord communicates in many different ways. Our Heavenly Father sees every aspect of our lives, yet He is always good.

> *Trust in the Lord with all your heart and lean not on your own understanding. In all your ways acknowledge Him, and He will make your paths straight.*
>
> Proverbs 3:5-6

THERE'S NOTHING WRONG WITH THE COLOR OF MY SKIN

BETH BOLDEN

"I am beautiful, I am wonderful, I am special and I am unique!" These are the words that my mother, Mrs. Marynette Reid Bolden, would have me chant as I stood in front of the mirror and combed my hair every day.

A positive self-esteem is needed in order for you to achieve what God has created and designed for you while you are on Earth. My mom addressed the issues of teasing and taunting very early in my life, as early as nursery school. Children told me I looked differently than them. Back then, children would try and guess the ethnicity of other children. Many times, they mispronounced the name. One day, I told my mom what my peers were calling me, and she corrected me and told me the correct pronunciation of the word. She told me that the other children were just upset because they envied my appearance.

This scenario encouraged me to discover why people say negative things about other people's outer appearance especially when the victim has not bothered anyone. I quickly realized it was easier to focus on positive words and expressions rather than dwell on the cause of people's actions. I soon realized that children and adults need to be redirected to God's Word and what it says about them. I realized that in my life's journey throughout school and my career, you can make a difference if you remain positive when interacting with others. This is not always possible and when it is not, you have the freedom to remove yourself from the situation. When you read the Bible and begin to mediate on what God's Word says about you, your inner spirit becomes strong, and you will not be moved by what others say about you. Surrounding yourself with positive people is also another way to remain positive and maintain a healthy self-esteem.

The world today is much different from the world I grew up in. Bullying is now a crime, and people can go to jail for threatening other people and name calling. I am currently an educator with over 20 years of experience. Name calling is still prevalent today in the school environment. On social media, students identify themselves with hashtag handles such as #TeamLightSkin and #TeamDarkSkin. Because of this, I wrote a children's book entitled, "There's Nothing Wrong with the Color of My Skin." Skin is the largest organ in the human body. It is important to understand the purpose and function of skin. The color of skin varies from person to person, but it does not interfere with its purpose.

Beloved, God's Word says in Psalm 139:14, "For I am fearfully and wonderfully made." Matthew 5:14 says, "You are the light of the world." 1 John 3:2 says, "We are children of God and we will resemble Christ when He returns."

These are God's Words to us. You see, this is the only identification you need: God's Word! You are beautiful, you are wonderful, you are special and you are unique!

When God says it that settles it! Go forth beloved, and do God's will for your life on earth because there's nothing wrong with the color of your skin!

You are all fair, my love and there is no spot in you.

SONG OF SOLOMON 4:7

HOW I SURVIVED THE LOSS OF MY MOTHER, MILLINEASE BUCHANAN

WINIFRED BONDS

My mother passed away on August 29, 1979, while showering at her home in Florida. Although we did not have an autopsy completed, she was recently treated for hypertension so the coronary attributed her death to a stroke. When my mother was a teen my great grandmother died in her sleep. So, it was a known fact that high blood pressure was hereditary on my mother's side of the family. In the 20s, 30s and 40s, my mother and her siblings were raised on a farm in South Georgia by their father. As a farm girl, my mother worked in the fields picking cotton, pulling corn, weeding the acres of crops and also cooking for the family.

My grandfather was a farmer and the sole provider for a family with nine children; money was scarce. Since there were no high schools for colored children, he managed to send most of his children to a nearby boarding school in Cordele, Georgia. My mother learned valuable skills at the boarding school such as sewing, cooking and other household-related duties. These skills served her well in life as a wife, homemaker and mother.

My mother met my father when she was a teenager. Out of their union came four children: three boys and one girl. Because my mother lost her mother at an early age, she desired to be the best mother possible. Even though my mother was a strong disciplinarian, she showered us with love.

From my mother, I developed a love for beautiful things such as flowers, art, clothes and decorations. My mother's attitude helped my siblings and I look past the point that we were poor. She taught us, "If life gives you lemons, make lemonade." During our childhood, we owned a vegetable and flower garden. I remember having to pick flowers from the garden at an early age. I made bouquets in a mason jar to decorate the living room and kitchen table.

In the 1950s and 1960s, we had a small TV that showed black and white pictures only. The TV station went off air by 8 p.m. All programming was geared towards the majority race in America. The two popular shows were, "Hee Haw" and "Grand Old Opry." Despite it all, my mother became very creative in stimulating us. We would take long walks in the woods, and she would identify trees and different plants. To this day, I can identify various trees and plants. My mother taught me how to sew, but she also taught me lifelong lessons. I learned how to keep my dignity when confronted with racism, how to keep my friends and loved ones close, and how to handle others "with a long handle spoon."

Over the years my mother and I became closer even after I had my own family. Despite what my mother had been through, she was my biggest supporter. There was even a time when my mother and father were run out of town by the Ku Klux Klan for assisting African Americans with voting in Georgia from 1961-1964. After my divorce, my mother was there for me. She allowed my children to spend summers with her in Florida. She consistently demonstrated how strong of a woman she was. In my mind, my mother was my super woman who would live forever. She offered my family love, emotional support and financial assistance when necessary.

Looking back, I don't recall asking my mother how she was holding up, or if everything was all-right until the night of August 28, 1979. She called to see if I received a box for my children. She was so thoughtful; she often sent them gifts. She sent jewelry for my daughter and suits for my sons. I can remember that night like it was yesterday. I asked my mother, "Are you all-right?" She replied in a strange voice that she just wanted the children to have those things. On my way to work the next morning, my whole world came tumbling down. My eldest brother waved me down as he drove towards me frantically. He told me my mother passed. We managed to pull ourselves together to prepare the funeral for our beloved mother. Her passing left me grieved and extremely sad. I felt as if I was going to die!

Three months later as I was driving down the highway, the pain was so great that I cried out for God to help me. I looked up in the sky as the clouds formed. There was a beautiful, unusual sight of the clouds parting as if God was speaking to me through the clouds. It was such a beautiful and peaceful sight that I began speaking in tongues. As a Baptist, this was something I had never done before. The car became saturated with the Spirit of God in and all over me to the point that I could not drive. I pulled my car over to the side of the road and submitted to the prompting of the Holy Spirit and let Him have His way.

Recently, Bishop Bronner taught from II Chronicles 20:5-12 and asked, "Where do you look when you get in trouble?" His response was, "Look to God first." Wherever you look first is where your faith is. At the time of my mother's passing, I didn't know what faith was. I eventually realized I depended on my mother for everything including her faith. Over the years, God has shown me that I need to seek Him for myself. To assist me, God put people in my path to help me spiritually evolve. I've challenged myself to get into the Word of God by reading my Bible more and listening to faith teachings. This is the legacy I want to leave my children and grandchildren. "Look to God first, that is where your faith is."

> *But seek first the kingdom of God and His righteousness, and all these things shall be added to you.*
>
> MATTHEW 6:33

JESUS MAKES THE UNBEARABLE – BEARABLE

ELIZABETH BOYKIN

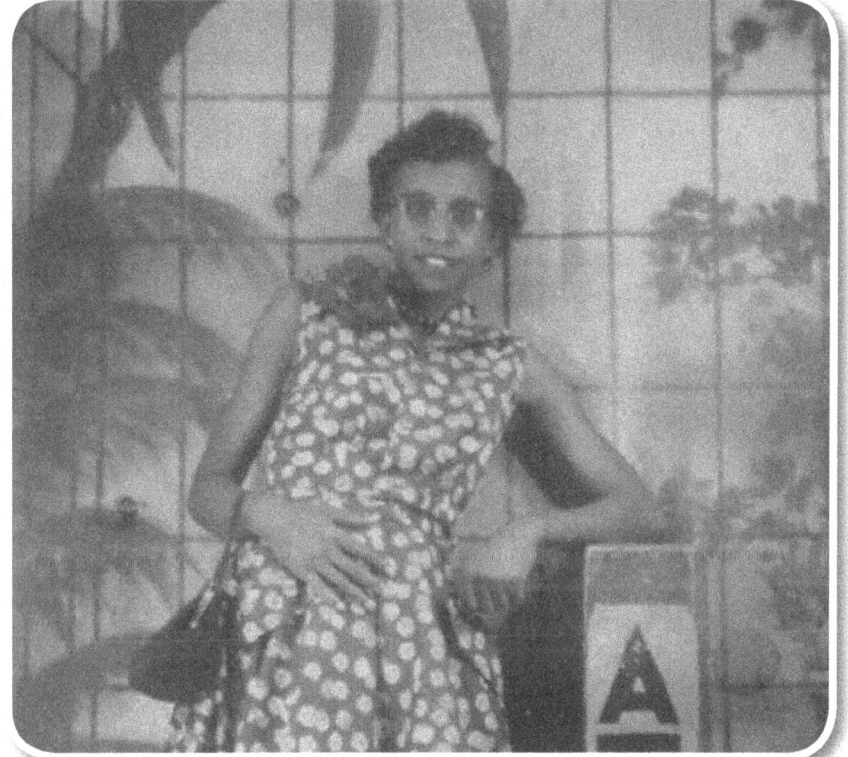

Elizabeth Boykin

My mom and daddy use to say, "Do unto others as you would have them do unto you," and, "If you can't say anything good, don't say anything at all."

I was raised in a very religious household; my dad was a minster. I married at a very young age, which I wouldn't advise to anyone unless you and your partner are deeply grounded in Jesus Christ. I held on to what my parents instilled in me, but I married the total opposite. There were good times but plenty of bad times. My husband was a great provider but not always a great husband. I often felt like his mother instead of his wife. He repeatedly cheated on me. There was no romance in our marriage, so I learned love and forgiveness. I prayed and cried a lot while having to raise our four children. My daughters witnessed so much and learned the dos and don'ts for marriages. I have three daughters, two of them are divorced and one never married. As a child, I was also taught that having any man is better than having no man. I loved my husband, but I did not like him at all. I stayed with him for 54 years through thick and thin. Even when he became ill from 2001 to 2003, I remained by his side. While he was ill, he asked God for forgiveness. He also asked me to forgive him for all of the years of infidelity. Because of the God I serve, I forgave him. Now my life is full. I don't live with any regrets. I live my life by the Word of Jesus Christ which carried me these 84 years. Always keep Jesus close! He is the husband that made my life bearable those 54 years.

FINDING CONTENTMENT IN EVERY SITUATION

KATE BOYKIN

How can you find contentment living with an unsaved mate? I assume there are many women dealing with this situation, because women outnumber men in many churches.

I met my second husband seven years after my first husband left. My first husband went to South Carolina to look for a better job. He never came back nor did he make any attempt to help support our two children. I filed for a divorce, and the court ordered him to pay child support. He seldom paid anything, and I didn't have the resources to hire a lawyer to hold him accountable. I struggled to raise two small children alone. I was eagerly searching for a husband and as a result, I became involved in unhealthy relationships.

At that time, I was not saved even though I went to church regularly. My aunt, who raised me and my three siblings after our parents died, took us to church every Saturday. She was a devout Seventh Day Adventist. When I was 12, I went to live with an older brother and his wife and their four children. We attended a Methodist church every Sunday, but I don't remember ever hearing a message about being born again, the Holy Spirit or being told to read the Bible. However, I read my Bible occasionally.

When I married my second husband neither of us were saved. I believed once I got married again, all my problems would be solved and for a while they were. We bought a home, and I purchased my first car. When we moved into our home, there was a small church in our neighborhood about two blocks from our house. It was vacant for several years. One day as I was passing the church, there was a pastor in the yard. I stopped and talked to him as he shared with me that he was getting ready to open the church. A few weeks after the church opened, I stopped by to check it out. He was a Pentecostal pastor, and I had never heard the Bible taught the way he taught it. He taught

Kate Boykin

about the Holy Spirit, speaking in tongues, tithing and how the Bible could relate to me in my daily walk with the Lord. So, I began reading my Bible more often. For the first time, I enjoyed going to church. I continued going, but I wasn't ready to make that final commitment. However, God had a different plan for me. In one of the evening services, I ended up at the altar weeping. That day, I gave my life to the Lord. That was the beginning of my walk with Him. My life and my values began to change as I grew in the Lord. I was so eager to learn more that I was in church every time the doors opened.

On the other hand, my husband had no interest in going to church. All three of our children went to church and eventually were saved. My husband and I were no longer on the same page. I began praying for his salvation. The most difficult thing has been living out my Christian journey alone and not having a mate to share those interests and experiences with. He continues to live his life as usual and has no interest in becoming a Christian. It's like we are married but traveling down two different roads. I have been praying for his salvation for thirty years and still believing.

I've learned that once I have done all I can, I should stand steadfast, unshakable, immovable in the Lord and be content in whatever situation I am in. I usually don't worry about things because I believe I can do all things through Christ who strengthens me. To keep myself busy, I have attempted to do many things. I love learning, and I have a passion for sewing. I make most of my clothes and have sewn bridesmaid dresses for many weddings. I have done alterations and made window treatments. I am also an excellent cook. God has truly been good to me and given me many talents. I know how to lay tile, hang wallpaper and paint. Since 2005, I've been a teacher and team leader with the Children Ministry at Word of Faith. The Bible says "train up a child in the way he should go and when he is older he will not depart from it." I love planting seeds and making an impact in the lives of children.

If it wasn't for the presence of the Lord in my life, I never could have made it. Even when I didn't know Him, He was directing my steps toward Him. If I didn't marry my husband and move to another neighborhood, I may not have gotten saved. It has all worked for my good.

Time and space will not allow me to give more details of my past. But I was raised without parents by my aunt and an older brother. I married the first time to a jealous and abusive husband who left me with two small children to raise. God is the only Father I've known, and He has truly been awesome. I have such contentment and peace, because my heart belongs to Him. He has given me peace that passes understanding. No matter what your circumstances are, be willing to lean onto God, serve Him and trust Him. Most of all be a committed tither and He will see you through any circumstance. I started tithing when I first got saved, and that's why God has been so good to me. I have sown seeds in the lives of others. The Bible says, "Give and it shall be given unto you; good measure, pressed down, shaken together and running over." I have gone on mission trips to Haiti, Jamaica, Alaska, Costa Rica, Italy, Columbia and New Orleans. I've been on cruises to Jamaica, Nassau, Key West and Mexico. I am content with living my life for the Lord.

No matter where you are on your life's journey, always believe that your latter days will be greater than your former days. Live each day with a positive attitude. To change your world, all you have to do is manage your thoughts and feelings. Your life will follow your thoughts.

> *Commit your works to the Lord, and your thoughts will be established.*
>
> PROVERBS 16:3

MARRIAGE MATTERS

PAUL AND INGRID CANTRELL

P roverbs 18:22 states, "He who finds a wife finds a good thing, and obtains favor from the Lord." Paul and I have been married for 34 years. We can truly say God has been more than faithful to us. We have learned throughout the years to trust Him more each day. We deeply love each other and our strong love for Jesus enables us to stick closer together as we journey through life. When you spend time with anything or anyone in life – it will reveal its secrets to you. The time we spend together studying God's Word and applying it to our lives has blessed our marriage.

For us, we put God first, family second and careers or our livelihood third. One day, we heard a couple who had been married more than 60 years say they never go to bed angry. We made that vow to each other, and we have kept that commitment. Also, we practice the following and invite you and your mate to join us.

- Hold each other's hand in the mall and in church.
- Tell each other, "I Love You" at least three times a day.
- Help the wife with household chores.
- Listen to each other for communication is very important.
- When possible, worship together at the same church.
- Be open about your saving and checking accounts.
- Have a date night at least once a week.
- Always pray together for there is power in agreement.
- Let each other know how good they look when dressing up.
- Express your appreciation for your mate.
- Give gifts unexpectedly.
- Little foxes spoil the vine; say what irritates you before it becomes a giant.
- When a blended family gets married-- include the two family members in the wedding so they can feel like a part of the family that is becoming one.

SETTLE NOT!

JACQUELINE CHAPMAN

I became pregnant with my first child at 15. If I believed the whispers I heard from my family members about my future, I wouldn't be in the position I'm in today.

When I was 13 years old, my mother was a single parent with ten children. I was the fourth child with six siblings under me. I witnessed my mother struggle, and I knew I didn't want to be in the same situation. However, by the time I was fifteen and in the 9th grade, I became pregnant. I quit school altogether. By the time I was 18, I was a single parent with two children and only a 9th grade education. I started to feel like I was on the same path as my mother; a road I did not want to travel. I didn't want to live as an adult with a house full of kids and a 9th grade education. With the help of public assistance, I moved out of my mother's apartment into my own.

The following year, I became employed part time at Bronx State Hospital. As time passed, my children started elementary school. By the grace of God, I got my first "break." My job began offering educational programs to employees during their work hours. This was a great advantage for me. My job setup an annex for the school program in the back of the hospital. The hospital partnered with Bronx Community College and Lehman College to offer GED classes as well as undergraduate courses.

I registered for GED classes immediately. I took the test a few times before I passed. I remember I took the test for a final time in July, and in my heart I knew I would be registering for college that

following September. I was so overwhelmed. I even made babysitting arrangements for my children, so I could attend class on campus.

I started with a two-year college because I needed to make up for not graduating from 9th grade and dropping out before attending high school (which included 10th-12th grade at the time). I no longer would have to lie about graduating from high school. While working on my first degree, I was offered a full time position at work. This enabled me to cancel my public assistance. It was a struggle, but I maintained going to work, school and raising my children.

I was finally getting to the point where things were getting better. Then, one day the apartment above me caught fire and destroyed my apartment forcing me to relocate to the projects. This setback confirmed that my income was insufficient. I needed to focus on finding a career or better-paying job. I completed testing for various city jobs and ironically, they all called around the same time. I chose New York City Department of Corrections because they offered the most pay. After being on the job for six months, I graduated with my associate's degree. Within a year, I moved out of the projects into my Co-Op apartment. I returned to school and graduated with a B.A. in Deviant Behavior and Social Control. While attending school, I was promoted to Captain, and several years later I retired. Because I was financially secure, I moved to Georgia.

A life lesson is that no matter what you go through in life, you may have to compromise but you do not have to settle. I went from being the example of what not to do to being the example of what hard work and dedication can do.

> *There is no passion to be found in settling for a life that is less than the one you are capable of living."*
>
> NELSON MANDELA

LIVING MY VISION

SHANDRA CHILDS-THOMAS

My mom and dad use to say, "God bless the child that has his own." They meant that, literally. I am from a family of twelve children. As the second oldest child, it was my responsibility to do chores daily, babysit my younger siblings and learn to sew. I have been sewing since I was 8 years old. Unlike kids today, if we wanted spending money, we had to earn it. My parents always said, "If you have education and a trade that you like, you will never have to worry about a job." They also stressed that using those skills and your creativity will afford you the finer things in life. Those skills are gifts from God that no one can take from you. However, you must use and share them.

Throughout the years, my family has learned valuable lessons from me and my mother. My mother created many of our clothes; she was an excellent seamstress. She also made absolutely beautifully matching outfits for my dad and herself. As you can imagine, money doesn't go very far when you are clothing twelve children. I've transferred those lessons with my children. Throughout my daughters' lives, I encouraged them to be the best at whatever they chose to do. I praise God for their success! Michelle has a lifelong position as a Federal Judge, and Tracey owns a healthcare business. God blesses the child that has his own.

In high school, I took home economics. I babysat during the summer to buy fabric and sewing supplies to make my outfits. In 1970, I became the Sunday School Activities Director for Church of the Master. For almost 10 years, I coordinated the sewing classes that designed the costumes for the children's plays. We also made fabric gift baskets and pillows.

Because of our excellent crafting skills, my two sisters and I began a business. My career experience includes: supervising customer service representatives, writing operating procedures for customer service, operating the furniture procurement department at Bell South and starting an interior design and custom workroom business after retirement.

In 1989, I moved to Atlanta, Georgia. I returned to college to pursue a career in interior design. Afterwards, I attended Atlanta Area Tech and learned to make draperies and window treatments.

Upon completion, I opened my own studio, Paradise Interiors, Inc. I offered a full line of interior design including space planning, model homes, renovations, remake, custom window treatments and bedding. I am honored to say that I've had 6 interns to work under me from Bauder College. They are all doing very well. One designer has followed my advice on furthering her career by expanding into the construction field of designing.

Sewing has truly been a blessing and definitely something I can share with others. I can design and make almost anything. I was very blessed to be able to instruct my workroom personnel on various custom creations for the home or office. I was able to team up with another interior designer to design most of John Weiland's model homes in South Atlanta. I also designed window treatments, decorated for Coca Cola and about five churches.

In 2003, I received a call from Bishop Dale Bronner's Administrative Assistant asking me to come to the office regarding the new church design (Word of Faith). After meeting with Bishop, I was given the job as principal designer and project manager. I went back to my car and cried--tears of joy, of course. A miracle happened. But then I thought, "How am I going to handle a project this large?" I prayed for God to send me the right team to work on the project with me. Within a week, I gathered my team and guess what – they were also members of the church, Word of Faith. The Word of Faith design project is the highlight of my career.

It was now time for me to start giving back. I always wanted to teach young children how to sew and I yearned to encourage people who were recently incarcerated or in a bad situation to learn a trade so they could be self-sufficient. Remember, God blesses the child that has his own. Since moving to Columbia, South Carolina in 2009, I have partnered with the Auntie Karen Foundation, and we have taught middle school children how to sew. They are so hungry for this gift that so many of us take for granted. These kids are extremely talented. It brings tears to my eyes when I see how happy they are doing something they enjoy. I am also working with a gentleman who was released from prison for drug possession. This person is so eager to learn. He has said many times, "There are people in prison who need a second chance." We are opening the doors to give them that second chance.

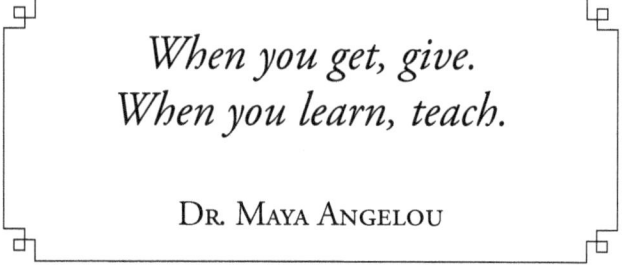

When you get, give.
When you learn, teach.

Dr. Maya Angelou

LOVE

REVEREND CLARICE W. CHURCH

1 Corinthians 13:13 states, "And now abide faith, hope, love these three; but the greatest of these is love."

The very essence of who I am can be described as one who loves every human being. I feel the love of God within me and through me.

My love is for everybody – man, woman, boy, white, black, brown, rich, middle class, poor, saved or sinner. Every human being has value including the homeless, the alcoholic, the drug addict, the imprisoned and those who have lost hope. Every person needs to be loved. God loves them, and so do I.

1 John 4:7-8 states, "Beloved, let us love one another, for love is of God, and everyone who loves is born of God and know God. He who does not love does not know God, for God is love."

I conclude with the memories of my mother and daddy who always made me feel loved. I remember as a child when I came home from school, I would go to the kitchen where I usually found my mother cooking dinner. Instead of permitting me to wash dishes or help prepare dinner, my mother would always tell me to go do my homework and study.

Now, as an adult and mother of two girls and two boys, my advice is: always strive for excellence in everything you do, and always work unto the Lord.

Remember, in Christ Jesus I love you, but God loves you more, because GOD IS LOVE.

Rev. Clarice Church

> *Let us always meet each other with a smile, for the smile is the beginning of love.*
>
> MOTHER TERESA

THE TURNING POINT

DOROTHY GIBSON COBB

Dorothy G. Cobb

Should I pursue a career as a librarian or school teacher? As a school-aged child, I loved going to the library to read books and to observe the librarian at work. "I want to be a librarian when I grow up," I often told my brother and sisters. Upon entering Spelman College, I took the required courses for a major in English and a minor in Elementary Education. Since many of my relatives were educators, they encouraged me to be prepared to teach even though I wanted to be a librarian. I dreaded the time for student teaching, because I had little interest in teaching.

However, student teaching was great sometimes. Having graduated from college, I was employed as a teacher in August of the same year. I spent the summer thinking about the first day of school. That day finally came!

The darling little children walked into the classroom, some smiling, others simply staring at me. Completing lesson plans, attending 30-minute lunches with the children, completing home visits, making assignment corrections and making teaching aids and reading teacher manuals on Saturdays and Sundays (after church) was too much for me! So, I decided to enroll in Atlanta University's School of Library Science as an exit strategy from the drudgery of teaching. I took classes after work hours. And, do you know what happened? Those little active, trusting, loving and caring children touched my heart! I thought about Matthew 19:14 where Jesus said, "Let the little children come to Me, and do not forbid them; for of such is the kingdom of heaven."

Being a librarian was not for me. Little did I know, I had found my God-given gift! Jeremiah 29:11 states, "I know the plans I have for you, declares the Lord, plans to prosper you and not to harm you, plans to give you hope and a future." Teaching was God's plan for my lifework.

I spent the next 36 years of my life in the classroom. During those years, I was grade level chairperson, a supervising teacher, and I received Teacher-of-the-Year, Excellence in Teaching, and Outstanding Service in Education awards. I also taught Sunday school for 14 years at Word of Faith Family Worship Center and the Cathedral. Now that I am retired, I am serving as Ministry Leader for Word of Faith's Voices of Light Children's Ministry.

A word of advice I would give to young people contemplating a future as I did is a thought from *The Sound of Music*:

"Climb every mountain, search high and low. Follow every byway, every path you know.

Climb every mountain, ford every stream. Follow every rainbow, 'til you find your dream. A dream that will need, all the love you can give, every day of your life, for as long as you live."

> *Cherish your visions and your dreams as they are the children of your soul, the blueprints of your ultimate achievement.*
>
> NAPOLEON HILL

A LEGACY OF LOVE

MATTIE COPELAND

A disciple is a student and a follower. Discipleship means that a person accepts the way of life that has been taught and demonstrates and applies it in all aspects of their life. I am the oldest of ten children and we were raised in a nuclear family. Each day I think of my mom, who is now 93 years old. As I recall all of the wonderful memories of my childhood, it brings great joy and fulfillment to my heart to know that I was reared and trained in a Christian family. My parents taught us to love God with all of our hearts, to treat others like we want to be treated and to take time to relax and enjoy our family.

"God directs injunctions to parents first of all, to nurture children," states Deuteronomy 6:6, 11:18-21. In Ephesian 6:4, Paul adds that parents must bring children up "in the training and instruction of the Lord." Ideally, children experience and develop their ability to live the Christian life within a secure family environment based on a Christian atmosphere of love and support. I sincerely hope to leave a legacy of knowledge of being in God's grace and to implement what the Bible says on how we should live and treat one another. The first agency of Christian nurture takes place in the home. Home is where daily interactions, discussions, devotions, provisions of toys, games, books, sharing, chores, going out together, and so on, happens.

However, sometimes this doesn't happen in families or the home. In those cases, it is my responsibility as a Christian to show the love of Christ in my daily life. When I humble myself to serve others, I consider them as one of God's chosen whether they are homeless or seeking a better way of life. 1 John 3:11 says, "For this is the message that ye heard from the beginning, that we should love one another." Truly, what the world needs is more love. Everyone is seeking love but in the wrong places. When I teach others how to love self

and others as Christ loves us, then love grows and spreads into other's homes, schools, workplaces and into the world. Jesus identified two commandments that are the greatest. Matthew 22:37-39 says, "Thou shalt love the Lord thy God with all thy heart, and with all thy soul, and with all thy mind." This is the first and great commandment. And the second commandment is, "Is like unto it, Thou shalt love thy neighbor as thyself." In order to love Jesus, we must believe in Him. When we do that, He promises that we will live in Him and He in us. The evidence of that is found in the Holy Spirit who dwells permanently in us. This is shown in our daily lives. I've made an effort to demonstrate the same principles and leave a legacy of love for my children, grandchildren and others whom I encounter daily. I pray my Christian modeling of Christ-like living will help the following generations.

I hope to leave a legacy of promoting a vision of the Kingdom of God. My goal is to leave a central understanding of Jesus Christ's teachings that is implicit in the Christians' mission statement of the Kingdom of God. If I can leave just half of the legacy my parents bestowed on me, future generations will be taken to great heights in their walk with the Lord.

Tell me, I'll forget. Show me, I may remember. But involve men, and I'll understand.

CHINESE PROVERB

A TEACHER'S STORY

IRIS DAVIDSON

Since age three, I remember my mother reading Bible stories to me. I can still see Mary on the donkey with Joseph out front leading the donkey. I was always amazed by the baby in Mary's arms. What a beautiful baby with rosy cheeks and a halo around His head. I knew this baby was special. My mother introduced me to Jesus Christ. At the time, I didn't realize how fortunate I was to have a parent who introduced me to the King. She was determined to plant this seed in my heart and point me in the right direction. My mother was such an awesome influence in my life, and she always served as a Sunday school teacher. This was perhaps the beginning of my desire to become a teacher. Whenever I played as a child I acted as the teacher, and I assigned work to my students while holding a ruler.

In 1973, I graduated from Spelman College with a degree in English and Secondary Education. Because I had a desire to further assist my students, I graduated from Georgia State as a Reading Specialist with a desire to become an excellent educator. This was not an easy task for me; however, I realize to whom much is given much is required. My learning experiences made me more and more aware of racism in Georgia, and it really hurt my heart seeing so many students fall between the cracks. As Bishop says, "Get all the education you can, and can all you get." My concern is: what am I doing to help my children? How can I help them? There are teachers from Atlanta Public Schools (APS) with integrity and love for their students. I wish more people were aware of the many times teachers bought shoes, clothes and food for students. We always took good care of them.

My past experiences helped me become the best teacher possible. I taught high school for 35 years at Frederick Douglass High School, and the principal and staff were wonderful. However, in 2009, the APS cheating scandal occurred. All teachers were not involved in the cheating scandal. And

Iris Jackson Davidson

please note that in my opinion--Atlanta is the only place where teachers have been lynched because of a standardized test.

Perhaps the test should have been on trial and not the teachers. Many of those teachers were not cheaters but very loyal and protective of our students. The test does more harm than good for many minority students. Even before the scandal, there were distasteful comments made by several professional teachers that our children suffered from Attention Deficit Hyperactivity Disorder (ADHD) and need medication. Many strategies were implemented by our staff to deal with behavioral problems; however, the trend continued with no consequences. Education continues to suffer in Georgia for public school students because of lack of leadership. I pray and encourage others to pray for better education for our children.

Currently, I teach at Atlanta Technical College, and I am so thankful God allows me to continue to work in education. Each semester I incorporate His love and reach out to my students not only with academics, but point the way to heaven and His glory. He is always on my mind, heart and soul. He gives me discernment, love and concern for those around me and gives me the opportunity to serve my family, coworkers and students.

> *Education is the most powerful weapon which you can use to change the world.*
>
> NELSON MANDELA

MY MOTHER'S PRAYERS

REV. EDNA DILLARD

Rev. Edna L Dillard

Church was truly wonderful on Thanksgiving Day in 1969. I was sanctified by our Lord and Savior Jesus Christ. He washed, sanctified and justified me that day. I haven't been the same ever since. He showed me who my mother was and the relationship she had with Him. I began to understand why my mother had an altar in our home. She had a picture of Mary and baby Jesus and a candle that she let burn during the month on the mantle over the fire place. Every day at noon, my mother prayed on her knees in front of the fireplace. She called each of our names. She used one of the rooms of our four-bedroom shotgun house as her prayer room. One day, my mischievous youngest brother decided to hit her on the backside with a bolo bat ball while she was on her knees. She didn't move or say anything. When she finished praying, she caught him, shook him good and told him not to ever disturb her during prayer. She was a faithful church member. She attended church every Tuesday, Thursday and Sunday night. The Pastor was an ordained mother.

Each service, my mother would line each of us on the altar. Mother Kelly would anoint us from head to feet while calling the name Jesus. We learned to say the Lord's Prayer every night on our knees. I learned later that one of our usual prayers was a prayer of repentance, "If I have wounded any souls today, if I have led one foot to go astray, if I have walked in my own willful way dear Lord forgive. Forgive the sins I now confess to thee, forgive the secret sins I do not see. Oh guide me, love me and my keeper be, dear Lord forgive." Another common prayer was, "Father lay me down to sleep I pray the Lord my soul to keep, if I should die before I wake, I pray the Lord my soul to take, if I should live another day I pray the Lord to guide my way."

My sanctified mother used the wisdom she knew to "train us up the way we should go." We attended a local Presbyterian church in the community. The church held vacation Bible school, camps, nursery school, provided a basketball court, playground with swings, and an after school program. I was baptized by sprinkling in the church. I was a member until I was sanctified and began to search for more of God's Word.

My mother was an usher. She wore a white uniform, shoes, stockings and cap. She named me after her, Edna. I was born on Mother's Day. Career wise, I am a Registered Nurse. For years, I wore a white nurse uniform, cap, shoes and stockings. It is a blessing that I received an anointing from my mother. She wrote me a short letter when I left home. It read, "Edna, the church is praying for you; don't forget to pray."

Years passed and one day I received a death diagnosis of finding out I had stage-four cancer. I could have died and left two children and a husband. I prayed fervent, sincere, persistent prayer, and I fasted as well. I depended on the praying habits my mother taught me. I stopped going to the doctor. I fasted seven days and nights without eating or drinking. It seemed as if I died the fifth day, I was unable to raise myself up. My confession was, for God I'll live and for God I'll die. Thankfully, God let me live to see my children grow up, and I was unfortunate with my marriage.

Now, I am an ordained Elder at Word of Faith Family Worship Cathedral. During my days as a school nurse, I met students in a classroom to discuss Jesus. The students were asked to invite other students to join our Bible Study Club. The principal allowed me to become the teacher and a sponsor of the club. The club president is now the pastor of Word of Faith Family Worship Cathedral. I have been favored by God to own a Group Home for the Elderly and Transitional Houses for the Homeless. My mother's prayers have saved me from many tragedies. Thank God for praying parents! I advise parents to cover their children with prayer before they leave home every day. Get a genealogy prayer book and write family names in the book. God promised to show mercy unto thousands of them that love Him and keep His commandments.

> *If my people called by my name, shall humble themselves, and pray,*
> *and seek my face, and turn from their wicked ways;*
> *then will I hear from heaven, and forgive their sin*
> *and will heal their land.*
>
> ~ 2 Chronicles 7:14

OUR DISADVANTAGE IS GOD'S ADVANTAGE

EVANGELIST CAROLYN DIXON

I remember feeling like I began life with a disadvantage. My disadvantage was shyness. To be shy means to avoid contact with others and having the inability to speak. My shyness lasted for years! It was a very painful time in my life. Why painful, you may ask? Imagine having lots to say but allowing timidity to rob you of freedom of speech. No matter how much I told myself, "Today is your day to speak," I just couldn't seem to get the words out. The pain was so great, because I knew there was so much more to me than I was able to verbally express.

It is important to know the difference between being shy and being quiet. Being quiet is not wanting to speak or not having anything to say at the moment. Being shy is having a desire to speak, but not having enough confidence to say it.

During elementary school and high school, I was too shy to even walk into the classroom. Once I gained enough confidence to walk into the classroom, I would sit in the very back without speaking the entire period.

My shyness even affected my ability to express my thoughts on paper. I would start writing and then erase, repeatedly. One day my teacher told me, "If you keep starting over, you will never finish." Eventually, I learned there is always room for correction, but the key is to get started. Now, I am able to express myself completely whether it's right or wrong, and once it's out, then I make the appropriate corrections. Because I truly believe you cannot correct that which you don't express whether verbally or on paper.

I overcame my shyness when I dedicated my life to the Lord. As Galatians 2:20 says, "...I no longer live, but Christ lives in me." My God, what a difference Christ will make in our lives if we just let Him in. The breath of God began to breathe on my insecurities, and timidity went out the window. I replaced fear with faith, and I found myself taking opportunities to speak up and out by living life out loud. God began to erase stagnation and every stumbling block sent by the enemy to keep me back. When God called me forth, He put His Word in my mouth and I began to learn of Him. God saw fit to call me into the ministry to erase every piece of shyness inside of me.

As of today, the largest crowd I've proclaimed the gospel of Jesus Christ in front of was 3,000 people in Nigeria. Since then, I've gone to London, England, Brussels, Belgium, Trinidad and Tobago, West Indies and Cape Town, South Africa. I allowed God to deliver me. Perhaps, you are reading this story saying to yourself, "I can identify with her testimony, and I'm ready to live my life out loud." I encourage you to commit every area of your life over to the master, our Lord and Savior Jesus, and watch Him make something beautiful out of your life too.

> *I beseech you therefore, brethren, by the mercies of God, that you present your bodies a living sacrifice, holy, acceptable to God, which is your reasonable service. And do not be conformed to this world, but be transformed by the renewing of your mind, that you may prove what is that good and acceptable and perfect will of God.*
>
> ROMANS 12:1-2

MAMA KNOWS BEST

ALICE EVANS

"If any of you lacks wisdom, you should ask God, who gives generously to all without finding fault and it will be given to you." James 1:5

I was the last pea in the pod to join the Robinson Clan. I was the seventh child. My siblings were much older and most had migrated to Chicago. As a little girl I traveled to Chicago by train with my sister who resided in Atlanta. My trip was very enjoyable. A few years later, my mother and I permanently relocated to Chicago to live with my brother and his family.

I graduated from DuSable High School in 1949. After graduation I had a career choice to make. I will tell you how my Mother instructed me, what I did and how I changed my career path to line up with what God placed in my heart as a child.

As a little girl I always dreamed of being a nurse. But before graduating high school I experienced the glitz and glamour of becoming a high fashion model by enrolling in the D and D Charm School. After that class, I enrolled in the Academy of Charm in a very upscale area known as, "The Loop," in downtown Chicago. While attending the academy I met many interesting people. I met celebrities and professionals from various walks of life. I met musicians, athletics, etc. as well as my dear friend, Dr. William H. Harris.

At that time I was focused on becoming a successful model. However, my mother, Mary Louise Robinson, had a vision and saw me going down a path of destruction and discouraged me from continuing with my modeling career. To please my mother, I enrolled in nursing school. A few years later, my mother and I moved back to Atlanta.

Upon my return I took more nursing classes but never reached the level I originally planned to reach. My dream was to be a psychiatric nurse. The places I worked included: Hughes Spaulding Hospital, Private Practice Nurse Assignments for Dr. R.P. Jackson, Egleston Hospital for Children,

Department of Defense at Fort McPherson, Georgia Nursing Department and for a short time Internal Revenue Service, as a clerk.

On November 11, 1958, I married Mr. Walter Evans and to this union, I gave birth to my beautiful daughter, Caron Sharise Evans. My mother lived with me until she passed in 1978 at age 90. She always gave me and my daughter sound advice and wisdom.

The moral of my story for young people today is to stay focused on your dreams. Do not get excited about the worldly glamour and people that are supposed to be important but are far from God. I thank God for my mother's vision. I was getting away from my Christian rearing and became too busy for church. I thank God for helping me see the light and realize, "Only what you do for Christ will last."

Through all my experiences, I learned that I must pray and ask God to give me wisdom in my life choices. There are many options, and some may not be good for us nor God's will for us. If we listen to that small, still voice within, we will make the right choices. God is the strength of my life.

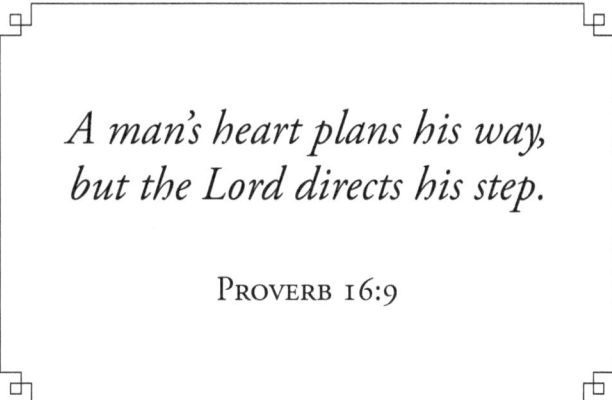

A man's heart plans his way, but the Lord directs his step.

PROVERB 16:9

THE ONLY SUITABLE SPOUSE FOR ME

JOHN GIBBONS

My story begins around 1992. A very good friend of mine, James Stiggers, invited me to church one day. Attending that one service was enough for me to know that Pastor Dale C. Bronner would be my spiritual shepherd and Word of Faith Church would be my church home. I joined Word of Faith the following Sunday after visiting. At the time, I was married to my ex-wife, so she joined as well. However that union would not stand the test of time; two years later we divorced. Although divorced, my ex-wife and I continued our service at the church. I worked on the video ministry as a camera operator and my ex-spouse worked on the hostess ministry. Eventually, she went on to worship at another church. I continued my video ministry service at Word of Faith for the next 10 years.

Fast Forward.

I remember why I joined Word of Faith; it was a wonderful atmosphere to learn about God and grow spiritually. When Word of Faith started a bowling league, I joined as a bowler. A lot of members participated – some that I knew, some that I didn't know. I was single at the time and had been previously married, so I was not looking for a relationship. However, there were many single ladies in the league. The one woman I noticed was Joyce. I would check her out without her or anyone else noticing me.

It wasn't easy to talk to Joyce during the tournaments, because everybody was focused on bowling, so I had to wait for my opportunity to talk to her. When it became time for our team to compete with her team, I made a connection with her. I asked her if she would like to receive some bowling lessons because I noticed she was struggling a bit during the game. She agreed, and we set up a time over the next few weeks to have practice sessions. We met one Saturday afternoon, and I taught her the art of bowling. She was very pleasant to talk to, and I began to see that she had a lot of qualities that I desired in a mate.

So, I suggested that we go on a date to get to know each other outside of bowling. We went to a small diner, and we talked and talked the entire time. We found that we had a lot of things in common such as raising a family, children being a high priority, etc. I started thinking to myself she would be a good candidate for a wife. Number one, we attended the same church and were receiving the same teachings from Bishop Bronner. Number two, we were both single. And number three, we were older and had been through a lot of difficult relationships. We were at a point in our lives where we were ready to take that step to move forward together.

After a few months of dating, we talked about marriage and the future and what we expected from each other. We agreed to exchange wedding vows. Joyce's family was very close, and I remember asking her mother, Ms. Lucille, for Joyce's hand in marriage. She said, "It is all right with me, but you are still going to have to ask her father." As Mr. Rayfield, Joyce's father approached us, Ms. Lucille walked away. I asked Mr. Rayfield if I could marry his daughter. He said he would have to think about it, I replied, "Okay," and headed home that evening. I found out later, during my absence, Ms. Lucille questioned Mr. Rayfield about my whereabouts. Mr. Rayfield told Ms. Lucille and Joyce, "John asked me to marry Joyce, and I told him I would have to think about it, so he left."

Now, rumor has it that Ms. Lucille chewed Mr. Rayfield out about the way he handled the proposal request.

Needless to say, mom and dad granted my wish of marrying their daughter. I proposed to Joyce, she accepted, and she put together a beautiful wedding ceremony in 2005. Her mother and father and loving brothers and sisters accepted me. Everything was perfect. After we married, we joined Word of Faith's first installment of Radical Love, and because we were newlyweds, we were indoctrinated with more information about love and marriage and spouse friendship for 12 weeks.

In 2005, we adopted a baby boy. In honor of my name, we named our baby boy Johnathan Andrew Gibbons. Johnathan is now 10 years old, and Joyce and I have been married for 15 years. We are still members of Word of Faith, and we are still very much in love and proud of our family.

Joyce has blessed my life tremendously! She has been supportive of my dreams. She has encouraged me to keep striving for my dreams, yet she has also chastised me when I get too full of myself. She continues molding and filling in gaps where Bishop Bronner has left off. She adds so much value to my life. The decision to marry her was the greatest decision I made my entire life. Our son, Johnathan Andrew Gibbons is the glue that holds us together. He is wonderful, gifted, loving, funny, loyal, helpful, friendly, courteous, kind, obedient, cheerful, thrifty, brave, clean and reverent. He is a Boy Scout!

We are growing together as a family unit, and we are getting the teachings that come out of the pulpit at Word of Faith. I love fatherhood. I love being a husband. I love my wife. I love my family. Our future is getting brighter each day. Joyce and I have shared so many ups and downs. Our marriage has been tested, and we survived with flying colors. There is nothing on the face of earth that will destroy this union as God is my witness. As for me and my house, we will continue to worship the Lord, God.

WHEN YOU LEAST EXPECT IT!

JOYCE A. GIBBONS

Joyce A. Gibbons

As a single woman, I experienced many ups and downs, challenges and disappointments in my past relationships. I felt that marriage and children was evidently not in God's plan for me. I often reflected on Jeremiah 29:11, "I know the plans I have for you saith the Lord … plans to give you hope and a future."

This is the story of how God blew my mind when I least expected it, and he will do the same for you.

By age 40, I had experienced a few bad relationships that left me emotionally drained and very discouraged. I always desired to be married, but it had not manifested in my life. I happily celebrated the engagements, weddings and baby showers of friends and family, while feeling a little disappointed that my turn had not come. One day, I decided I felt sorry enough for myself, so I stopped looking at being single as something to be embarrassed or ashamed about. It was time for me to heal and regain my strength.

My first step towards emotional healing was sitting in a quiet place with pen and paper. I wrote specifically what I wanted in a mate. I also listed the things I considered to be, "deal breakers." You see, I wanted a mate who had no children, because I experienced "baby mama drama" in a past relationship. I didn't want to have to deal with that in my next relationship. My friends said I was being unrealistic, because most men have children by age 40. However, their opinion didn't matter to me. This was how I felt in my heart. I prayed over what I wrote down and tucked the paper away in my Bible. At the time, that seemed to be an odd thing for me to do but creating that list gave me peace.

I put dating out of my mind and focused more on my court reporting career. Things were going great! I was meeting many new people, and the work was very rewarding! It kept me so busy that I had no time to dwell on the fact that my personal life was stagnant.

One day while I was out shopping, I purchased a bowling ball, shoes and a bag just because they were on sale. I had no definite plan to use them any time soon. A few weeks later, an announcement was made in church about joining the Word of Faith Church's bowling league. I thought, "Wow, perhaps this would be just what I needed to bring some fun into my life." I joined the league and brought my sister along with me on Friday nights for moral support. Bowling was a lot of fun, but I was not very good at it. After bowling for about three months, it was obvious that my skills were not improving. I really needed help!

Seeing how discouraged I was becoming because of my poor performance, my sister suggested I ask one of my league members named John to give me lessons. John was a tall, handsome, single brother who was our league's top bowler. He offered to work with me earlier, but I declined his help. I thought, "He is so good. Why would he want to waste time helping me?" Finally, I put my pride aside and asked for his help.

It was the beginning of a new year, January 2001. John and I started practicing on Saturday evenings, John was focused and committed to helping me improve my bowling skills. There was very little kidding around. Even though he was a tough instructor, I enjoyed taking lessons from him. Over the next few weeks, my bowling improved. Also, my friendship with John was growing. What started out as a teacher/student relationship was developing into something more. The odd thing was, we were both oblivious to what was happening.

For the next few months, we spent many hours talking about our childhood, relationships, successes and failures. I was comfortable discussing my innermost thoughts with him, and he seemed to feel the same way. One night in March, I reached to grab my Bible off my dresser, and my list of preferred male qualities fell out. I was brought to tears as I read the list. John had <u>ALL</u> of the qualities I listed, including having no children. I couldn't believe it. I thought, "God, can this be real?"

We continued to spend time together sharing our hopes and dreams with each other. In May of 2001, I received the surprise of my life when John proposed. I said, "Yes," but, it all seemed like a dream. I was expecting someone to wake me up at any moment. Needless to say, I was not dreaming. We began seriously considering spending the rest of our lives together. John was adamant that no wedding date would be set until we completed premarital counseling offered at our church. We both were a little apprehensive, because of the craziness we experienced in our pasts. You see, John had been married before, and this would only be my first marriage. By our second counseling session with Rev. Garmon, it was clear to all of us that God had brought us together.

We couldn't wait any longer. The date was set and we married on November 10, 2001 at our church, where we both attended for over ten years. It was hard to believe how God moved me from being single in January to being married in November of the same year. 2001 was a big turning point in my life. Our paths didn't cross until God led me to the bowling league.

For five years, things were wonderful. John and I enjoyed dining out, traveling and hanging out with friends. However, we felt something was missing. We desired to have children but thought it was too late. Little did we know God was not finish with us. In 2006, we were blessed with a beautiful baby boy we named Johnathan Andrew. Our circle was now complete. It has been 15 years and counting, and life is wonderful. God definitely blew our minds when we least expected it. He caused our paths to cross, and it is better than anything I could have imagined.

My advice to my single sisters over 40 is: do not despair. God has not forgotten you. He has plans for your life. When you least expect it, God will present you to your Boaz. You won't have to change a thing about yourself. He will love you unconditionally just the way you are. Be blessed!

LIFE VISIONS REALIZED

BETTY A. RICE GIBSON

Betty Gibson

It is a blessing to realize some of the dreams and life visions that one desires. Through this first person narrative, I will share some of my adventures of living in Liberia, West Africa. I was blessed to live a healthy, long life achieving some of my heart's desires. I hope by sharing my story, you will reminisce about precious memories from your life.

Over 50 years ago on the campus of the University of Kansas Jayhawkers, I celebrated my Fourth of July birthday. On that particular birthday, I introduced my younger brother Johnny to a student named Eleanora from Liberia. In May of 2015, Johnny and Eleanora celebrated their 50th wedding anniversary. My adventure begins with that introduction. Eleanora's family and friends were so impressed with my brother John that they inquired as to whether he had any sisters. He did and it was me.

From that introduction, I met my future husband, Lt. Col. Robert Henri Gibson II, Commander of the Executive Mansion Guard Battalion. His battalion was responsible for the protection of the President and the first family of Liberia. They were also responsible for welcoming dignitaries for the President. Where did I ALWAYS want to go and visit? AFRICA! From that introduction over fifty years ago, I began a new adventure which provided me over 43 years of experience I never imagined. I also met President Tubman and dined with him, his wife and other government officials at various functions. Eventually, my husband became a General. His promotion saved his life, because the officer who replaced him was killed early during a Liberian coup. After the military coup, my sons and I returned to the United States in 1980. My husband was unable to permanently join us as a family in California until about five years later.

As a child I had a strong interest in animals. I wanted to become a veterinarian. During Career

Day at my high school, I spent the day in a Veterinarian's office. The movies, "Born Free," and "Christian," were my favorites. They were about lions that were reared by humans, later released into the wild and returned to visit their human families. Growing up, our family had several pets; however, I fantasized about owning a real large pet cat. I purchased a Black Panther lamp and also created a book blurb about a big cat I named Tykayee. In Africa, I actually held a real baby tiger and was told I could have it. I also took my students to visit an animal owner in the wild who allowed us to handle his snakes and various other animals. In the States, I took my students to the petting zoo. Also, one of my husband's friends owned a large pet chimpanzee which the students played with, and he wasn't caged. Later, the chimpanzee put his hand out for me to shake it! As I shook his hand, he bit me and it required my husband and his friend to pull the monkey off of me. Chimpanzees are very strong, and we definitely did not become friends after that event.

Basically, the Liberians were very friendly. They spoke their dialects as well as English, but we were not always able to understand each other. We had memorable experiences such as a snake running into our home, and we were unable to find it for several days. When it was finally found, we were happy. One day, some fishermen brought seafood to our home and a large crab got loose around the house. I enjoyed going to shops to purchase masks as well as other African art. It was also interesting to watch the craftsmen carve beautiful designs in the tusks, but I learned that was death to the elephants even though some people ate elephant meat. Once in a while, someone in the Peace Corps would visit. One year, Bob's oldest sister spent time with us and created a beautiful quilt for us using long wooden blanks.

Living in Liberia opened the door for me to teach one year at a private primary school and about 10 years at the American Cooperative School. I believe the American and Liberian governments collaborated to provide an educational facility that offered grades Pre-K to 12th grade. The school had an international and professional faculty and staff. The student body was mostly composed of students from the ambassadors of the various embassies around the world assigned to Liberia.

As a classroom teacher, I didn't see any German, Japanese, Indian, Italian, African, French, Hispanic, Israeli, Korean or American children. However, the students were interested in learning languages different than their own. For example, some students enrolled in French lessons taught by a French teacher. I was able to see beautiful children happily creating art under the guidance of a genuine artist and also some inquisitive children discovering math solutions from an engineer. I recall one day when a group of cheerful children selected a name for a newly-born German shepherd that one of the students brought for me. If love, peace, harmony, joy and hope can exist in international classroom settings, why can't they exist in all environments?

At the end of the year, I was indeed touched when an Israeli family invited me to their home for dinner. They were pleased with their son's progress in my class. Initially, he was unable to speak English, but I utilized his classmates as well as students in the upper grades to help him learn English.

One activity that I'm sure many of us enjoyed at the American Cooperative School was International Day. On that day, the staff, students and parents from various cultures dressed in their native attire and shared a favorite dish from their culture. Because I was inspired, years later I helped my son's high school in the U.S. plan an International Day Program. Another activity we enjoyed was outdoor sports such as baseball games with faculty competing against students. The individuals who decided not to participate in the game were cheerleaders. The goal was to win by playing harmoniously. Do such things still happen in schools today? Also, does administration, faculty and staff still openly play and socialize as sincere friends together?

Also, while teaching, I was selected to attend a special International Conference held in Nairobi, Kenya with the Superintendent, his wife and a school board member. The board member who invited me was a missionary who taught a weekly Bible study in our home. My hope was to go to Africa, but I was blessed with that and more. After living in West Africa for 14 years, my school sent me to East Africa for a field trip. I went on a safari in Nairobi and slept on tree tops. At night, we watched wild animals come in huddles to the water below to drink. During our trip, we also visited other interesting places. Upon returning, I shared our experience via a presentation.

Let me share just one more experience while in Liberia. I met and became friends with missionaries from the Sudan Interior Mission (by the way, we still stay in contact). Several of those missionaries held a weekly evening Bible study in our home. A few of the faculty members from the school also attended. Eventually, I also organized the Gibson Good News Neighborhood Club where the children in our neighborhood and others would meet on Sunday afternoons. Students from Child Evangelism Fellowship who were trained by missionaries would come and teach Bible lessons on flannel boards. The children were also taught songs by the minister's wife who was a musician. She also taught our ladies Bible class. Usually on the fourth Sunday of the month, missionary friends came and showed the children a Christian movie. Holidays were celebrated with games, gift bags and goodies for the children.

After teaching in Kansas, West Africa and California, I was sent to an educational conference in Atlanta. I loved it. So, after I retired, my son and his fiancée helped me move to Atlanta, "the city in the forest." It was through patience and a labor of love that the Atlanta realtor, who sold us our home, found us a minister to bless our new home. Our agent attended Word of Faith and "lived her values every day. I was inspired and decided to become a member of Word of Faith Family Worship Cathedral as well.

My old vision board still stands in my bedroom. Another vision of mine is to become a successful entrepreneur. I was the oldest member of the July 2010 Bronner Business Institute NxLeveL graduating class. Please check out our website at www.AngelofVirtues.com.

After about 7 years, I reached my goal of finishing a book just before my 75th birthday. It is entitled, "Values for a Peaceful-caring World." My book is copyrighted, but not published. I sincerely hope that God has some meaningful purpose for these projects I felt led to complete.

I still have hopes, and I imagine we all will until we die. I realize that many of my hopes and desires have been fulfilled. I hope yours have and will be fulfilled too! Some of my experiences have allowed me to become a better and more informed individual. I would regret not having those same experiences. Presently, I wish for even better experiences for my children, my family and others.

Note: My favorite Bible scripture is Proverbs 3:5-6 from the Amplified Bible which I became familiar with in Liberia, "Lean on, trust, in and be confident in the Lord with all your heart and mind and do not rely on your own insight or understanding. In all your ways know, recognize, and acknowledge Him and He will direct and make straight and plain your paths."

Write the vision and make it plain on tablets, that he may run who reads it. For the vision is yet for an appointed time; but at the end it will speak, and it will not lie. Though it tarries, wait for it; because it will surely come, It will not tarry.

HABAKKUK 2:2-3

A DETERMINED LIFE

GLORIA A. GLASS

My life is very simple. I grew up in the Deep South around the time when Harry Truman was President of the United States. I grew up in the Old Fourth Ward Area. It was one street over from Sweet Auburn Avenue where Dr. Martin Luther King, Jr. grew up. The Old Fourth Ward is one of the oldest neighborhoods in Atlanta. My mother, Thelma Andrews, was a single parent. She took my sister Sandra, my brother Jerry and I to live with my grandmother, Amanda Johnson. My grandmother helped raise us until she passed. In the South during the 60s, due to racism, Blacks were separated from Whites by law. Blacks weren't able to eat in the same restaurants as Whites, drink from the same fountains, use the same public restrooms, attend the same schools, ride in the front of the bus or purchase a home. There were peaceful marches and racial disturbances that happened all over the United States of America.

Our family moved to College Park, Georgia, and that's where I met my husband, Robert Glass. I was friends with one of his sisters, Sandra Ruth. One day Sandra and I were walking in her backyard and Robert was already in the backyard. I never will forget what he said to me. He asked, "What's your name?" I told him. Then, he said, "You are going to be my wife one day!" I looked at him and thought to myself, "He is crazy!" Well as time went on, I did become his wife. Through our love, we had a son, Terance Glass.

We moved frequently until we finally settled into an apartment in Northwest Atlanta. That was a turning point in my life. My husband I were longtime friends with John Henry and Willie Kate Todd. They were just like family to us. We partied and drank together. Kate started going to this Holiness church called Galilee Holy Temple. She would ask me to join her, and I would always put her off or make up an excuse. One day, I finally went. I sat on the last row in the back of the church. During that service, I tried but failed to hold back the tears. The next thing I knew, I was at the altar crying and asking Jesus Christ to come into my life. I was so tired of the life of sin I was living, the same ol' same ol'. That night, I became a changed person; all the burdens I had were lifted off my shoulders. All the heaviness, habits, fears and wrong living was gone from my life. From that day on I wasn't the same. I began going to church regularly. Every time the doors opened, I was there. I became hungrier for God. I started to seek Him for the gift of the Holy Ghost. I wanted it more than anything. During my first visit at Kate's church, there was a visiting evangelist Prophet, A.A. Wilson. He was running a revival that morning. That man of God laid hands on me and prayed for the infilling of the Holy Ghost as he spoke in tongues. Everything was brand new, including me. What joy and happiness! I went home after church and told my husband that I received the gift of the Holy Ghost.

Soon after, I began working in the church on the usher board, in the choir, reaching out in the community, knocking on doors and inviting people to church. Then, one day the Lord called me to preach His Word. At first, I ran from the call. But, I knew it was the voice of the Lord, so I started studying God's Word and seeking His face for the anointing. Acts 5:29 says, "We ought to obey God rather than man."

Years later, my family and I moved to the Adamsville Community and became first-time home owners. Robert and I built a life and took care of our family together, while dealing with ups and downs along the way. Robert suffered from hypertension for a long time and one day, he developed a cerebral hemorrhage of the brain and died instantly. We were married for 27 years because of our relationship and love we had for each other.

After he passed, I didn't feel alone. I felt at peace in my heart, and I continued to do God's will.

The Lord Jesus Christ has used me in many areas of ministry.

"There was a 26 year-old man in critical condition that had a tumor on the stem of his brain causing him to have a stroke, three surgeries and a feeding tube in his stomach. I visited him and prayed the prayer of faith for him to be healed and led him through the sinner's prayer, to receive Jesus Christ as his personal Savior. Months later, God raised him up. Now he's walking and talking on his own. God performed a miracle. Hallelujah."

"Once there was a 40 year-old woman who was bit by a spider. She ended up in the hospital after experiencing symptoms of weakness and swelling. She was in and out of the hospital, because she couldn't get a proper diagnosis. Eventually, the doctors found that blood was not getting to her heart and she only had five pints of blood in her body. Her diagnosis was a myxama tumor, a rare heart disease. I went to the hospital to pray the prayer of faith over her believing God would raise her up from her bed of affliction. I anointed her with oil in the name of Jesus Christ. She underwent open heart and bypass surgeries. Through the miracle of praying in faith, she is still here, thanks be to God."

I give God all the glory honor and praise that his hand is on my life. It's his grace and mercy! As time goes on, I find that there is nothing simple about my life. I've learned how to let the peace of God rule and reign in my life. I am the woman of God he has called me to be in the service of the Lord.

> *Also I heard the voice of the Lord, saying:*
> *"Whom shall I send, and who will go for Us?"*
> *Then I said,*
> *"Here am I! Send me.*
>
> ISAIAH 6:8

CHRIST IN THE CRISIS

LILLIAN GRAY

In the summer of 2005 my year was going pretty well. I spent much time at the church putting together an instructional manual for our annual Koinonia Week which is very similar to Vacation Bible School. It was almost time to plan for the event that would take place in July. With only three weeks before Koinonia, there was pressure on the committee to complete the final details of meal planning, classroom schedules, teacher selection, training, etc., and I still had a lot to do myself.

One typical day after doing some work around my home, I felt a lump in my right breast. I was surprised and concerned, so the next day I immediately called to set up an appointment for a mammogram. That mammogram showed an abnormality, and a biopsy revealed Ducal Carcinoma in Situ in my right breast. "What is that? Speak English to me!" I thought. Then, I heard those three words you never want to hear, "You have cancer." I was diagnosed with stage 2 Invasive Carcinoma Breast Cancer on June 29. When I received the news, I was there alone and overwhelmed with fear and uncertainty. I remember feeling numb and wanting to deny the truth. It was such a confusing time that it didn't quite dawn on me how serious it was until I went through all the testing to prepare me for the fight of my life. I remember praying, "God, you've got to help me! I am overseeing Koinonia this year, and I'm a Sunday school teacher. I have a job… I have to work. I don't have time for this!"

How do you stand when you don't understand?

After all the questioning and much prayer, I began to experience the peace of God and the courage to fight for my life. Joshua 1:9 states, "Have I not commanded you? Be strong and of a good courage; be not afraid, neither be thou dismayed." Now, I had to deal with all the information that was thrown at me and learn about cancer, so I could make the right decisions.

The time came for all the tests, and I mean tests *and* procedures! My doctors recommended I

take chemotherapy first, then the surgery. I was, however, extremely resistant to the thought of chemotherapy, being nauseated often and of course the, "*Chemot**HAIR**apy*" thing! This was the hardest thing I ever had to do in life.

However, nothing prepared me for what was ahead. All of this was happening during Koinonia Week at church and oh yeah, I was still teaching Sunday school! I scheduled my first chemo the week after the activities at church. It was one of the most difficult three months of my life. By the grace of God, I made it through.

Before the battle was over, I endured 12 rounds of heavy-duty chemotherapy treatments, received a lumpectomy to remove the cancer and underwent 38 rounds of radiation. There were moments when I felt like I was in a deep, dark pit and could not climb out. Words of encouragement and prayers from friends, my church and biological family helped guide me to thinking positive thoughts. I gratefully received a Word from my pastor and bishop that the sickness was not unto death. I took that Word and ran with it! I stood on the scripture, "For I will restore health to you and heal you of your wounds." Cancer helped open my eyes to see that every day is a gift from God.

A year after fighting cancer, in June 2006, I began experiencing fatigue and shortness of breath. I ended up in the hospital emergency room. Several tests revealed I was in congestive heart failure and needed immediate surgery. The news was so surreal! I couldn't believe that I was critically ill and was unaware of it. Within days, I experienced open heart surgery to repair a mitral heart valve. After surgery, I began to experience complications and was told by my cardiologist that I developed a blood clot in my chest and would have died if I had gone home. All the while, I reflected on God's promises and read healing scriptures every day to sustain my faith, and He moved on His Word. I truly am a miracle woman. God healed and delivered me from death from cancer and open heart surgery.

My near-death experience intensified my appreciation for life. I celebrated in June 2015; it had been 10 years since my cancer diagnosis and 9 years since my heart surgery. There are so many people to thank for support and prayers. Looking back, I realize I learned a lot from my experience. Most importantly, I learned the power of God, patience, gratitude, humility and laughter. I choose every day to be grateful. My message: Listen to Your Heart….Trust Your Journey….Do Something. I know there is a reason for everything, and I believe I went through these experiences to give hope to others. I am very blessed to live this life and share my story with others. I am not merely a survivor; I am so much more.

Your Word is a lamp to my feet and a light to my path.

Psalm 119:105

28 DAYS LATER...

GREG GREEN

On Saturday, August 16, 2008, I prepared to leave for work. It was around 6:30 a.m. I was excited to leave that morning, because I finally added the bells and whistles on my motorcycle. It was a great looking bike, sleek, full of chrome and freshly waxed! I named my bike, "The Truth." Based on the weather conditions, it was the perfect day to ride. I chose a route different than my usual. I rode I-20 East from Douglasville to Atlanta and merged onto I-85 North. Man, I was moving and enjoying myself! As I began to exit onto the I-85 North ramp, I glanced at a green car about a half mile before passing it. As I attempted to exit, I noticed that traffic was stopped about halfway down the ramp due to construction. I began to downshift so I could stay to the right of the exit to detour south and then go north on another exit. I slowed to about 30 mph and suddenly "BOOM!" I was struck from the rear!

The impact was great. My head snapped backward. Everything seemed to be in slow motion. I took flight, almost like the bike was snatched away from me! I was in the superman flight position as I hit the pavement, sprawled out and slid for what seemed an eternity. It felt like I was trying to get to my feet before the slide was over. This reminded me of playing basketball when you stumble and while falling, you are still trying to get to your feet, before you finish falling, to make the play. Thank God, the lane I slid in was free of other vehicles! Miracles do happen! I remember standing up on my own and talking out loud to myself, "Did that just happen to me? Where is my bike? This can't be real!"

I smelled oil. A car pulled up, and a man asked, "Are you okay?" Still dazed, he got me to the roads shoulder and called 911. It is amazing how a person's senses have priorities. All of my focus was on the constant self-questioning. I didn't pay attention to the cars that slowed down while passing the accident, which caused traffic to back up. I heard sirens. I remember the ambulance coming and the paramedics tending to me. A police officer came to talk to me as I sat in the ambulance. One of the EMTs gave me a shot because of the shock from the accident. It helped me be in a mellow state. I just knew that everything was going to be all right. The driver of the car that struck me came to the ambulance to see me. I don't remember her name. I only remember that she was young and visibly shaken. I found out later that she was the driver of the green car I passed on the highway! My intentions for passing her were to avoid an accident. I spent a few hours at Grady Hospital. The priority to be treated was based on the severity of a patient's condition. While waiting to be seen, I saw some pretty messed up folks!

The medical staff thoroughly examined me. I survived the accident with no broken bones, a lot of rode rash on my hands, arms, legs, and a little whiplash. Thank God, I was released on the same day. However, I was very sore for the next few days, and of course, I had no bike! The thought of ever riding again held me with a gripping fear. I kept replaying the accident in my mind. I could still smell the oil that leaked out of my bike and the rubber on the pavement. A week after the accident, a friend took me to the salvage yard to retrieve the remains of my bike. I was wowed. It was mangled and a piece of the car's fender was lodged in the frame of the bike! I got my things out of the saddle bags and left my totaled steel horse. Even when I looked at my bike in photographs, I was still in fear and could smell the oil on the pavement.

One day, I saw a bike that caught my eye. It was in Chattanooga, Tennessee. A friend drove me to Tennessee to see the bike. I liked what I saw at the dealership. The dealers tried their best to accommodate me. Everything was falling into place except my fear. The salesman asked, "Do you want to test ride sir?" I responded, "Uh, no thank you. Just looking!" I stayed there about three hours, and then it hit me that my past accident was over, and if I didn't overcome my fear, I would never ride again. I started the process of purchasing the bike. *Uh Oh! I can smell the oil again!* All went well, and before I knew it, I was standing over the new steel horse putting my helmet on. I saddled that brand new VTX-1800 and returned home. The date was September 13, 2008, 28 days after the accident! Praise God!

> *Who controls the past controls the future. Who controls the present controls the past.*
>
> GEORGE ORWELL

PRETTY

JULIA COPELAND GREEN

My grandmother once told me, "It's hard for a pretty woman to have a man." I was about 11 years old at the time, and I did not understand. I was accustomed to being told I was pretty, but this was the first time I was hearing that my prettiness may not work in my favor. So, I asked my grandmother, "Why do you say that, Grandma?" She replied, "Because, you don't know if he loves you because he loves you, or if he loves you because you're pretty!"

Later, the consequences of my choices in life taught me exactly what my grandmother meant. At age 18, on August 7, 1999, I decided to get married. I was married for seven years. During the course of my marriage, I learned the true meaning of unconditional love. The love that I received during that marriage was based on conditions. Eventually, I realized that I had a choice. Either I could remain in a condition-based marriage with the conditions being control and manipulation, or leave the marriage and trust God. At the time, I was a 25-year-old student who was financially dependent on my husband. This was a tough decision to make, but I trusted God.

I have learned that being a pretty woman means I have a choice. Do I want to be with a man that says he loves me right now, or do I want to wait for the man that God has ordained for me? Five years after my divorce, on August 25, 2012, God blessed me with a husband, a husband that has loved me unconditionally. Just as Boaz said to Ruth in Ruth 3:10, " …Blessed be thou of the Lord, my daughter: for thou hast shewed more kindness in the latter end than at the beginning,

inasmuch as thou followest not young men, whether poor or rich." When my husband, Greg, and I were dating, he asked me, "Why are you interested in me? You can have any man you want! You could marry a rich doctor! Why would you choose to be with me?"

My response was, "Why can't I choose you?" I call Greg, "My Boaz Blessing," because he is a gracious gift from God.

In honor of Mrs. Lula Mae Copeland, my grandmother. Pretty is as pretty does!

HE NEVER SAID HE WAS SORRY

PAULA PALMER GREEN

About five years ago, I headed north on Highway I-85 in route to work. For some strange reason I reflected on my father. Tears streamed down my face as I said to myself, "He never said he was sorry." He passed more than 20 years ago. I thought I made peace with my past as it related to his absence and alcoholism, but I hadn't.

My parents were married, but mom left dad when I was about two years old. I'm thinking he probably got drunk, stayed out all night and failed to bring money home to pay the bills for the last time. Maybe it was the last time mama could bear. My uncles put me, my mom and my brother on the Greyhound bus from Yonkers, New York, to Bluefield, Virginia, to stay with my maternal grandparents.

My mom worked odd jobs in Virginia and eventually left us with our grandparents. She went back to New York to work and make a home for us. During that time daddy returned to Virginia, which was his hometown too. I remember the day he came to my grandma's house to see me and my brother. I thought he was so handsome. His skin was the exact color of my favorite candy, Hershey's bar. He had a square jawline; slicked-back wavy hair with the help of Murray's Pomade and a beautiful smile to boot. I was smitten with my daddy.

Through the years, he was in and out of my life. He was the type of alcoholic that would clean up, get a good job, stay sober and even preach from the pulpit for months on end. Then all of a sudden the urge would hit him to get back off the wagon. At age 6, my mom came to Virginia to get me and my brother so we could start school. We moved back to Yonkers, New York, and life was good. I started school, made friends and didn't hear anything from dad.

Ironically, one day he showed up. He was back off the wagon. We stayed in a four-story house. As I headed out to school one morning, I found my dad curled up in the corner on our porch. My heart skipped a beat, and I ran to tell my mom. By this time my mom had remarried and my stepfather politely asked him to leave. He left, but he also left a bad taste in my mouth.

For months he hung around our community. I believe he stayed at the Yonkers Gospel Mission Homeless Shelter. I remember one day going to the post office to mail a letter and he was sitting in front with a few of his other drinking buddies. Seeing him in that state made my heart rush and my feet run. I ran as fast as I could in the opposite direction hoping he would not call my name.

Eventually, he left New York and headed back to Virginia. Years passed and we would talk off and on. When he wasn't drinking, I liked him. I even loved him. He was an avid reader, great conversationalist and a Bible scholar. But when he was drinking I didn't want any parts of him. Deep down inside, I think he knew just how I felt. As the years passed, the drinking eventually stopped. He stuck with his Alcohol Anonymous meetings. I believe he was on a certain medication that made him sick if he drank. He remarried a very nice lady and they made a nice home together. I visited them and got to know my dad a little better. He was a smart, witty and charming man. I still cherish many beautiful letters that he wrote me and I shall have his tattered Bible. also I have a Bible he gave me. Stamped inside the Bible is: "Yonkers Gospel Mission," which is where he stayed on occasions. Since the organization gave my dad somewhere to lay his head, I often donate to that charity.

As his years came to an end, too soon, I asked him, "Why did you drink?" He said while sitting in his lazy boy with a pipe in his mouth, "I don't know." I miss him. I'm sorry he didn't get to meet his grandson. I pray that while the curse affected my brother and tried to get me, it won't touch my son.

Throughout the years, we would talk about salvation. He knew I hadn't been baptized. In my 30s I went to visit him. During that visit, I learned about his terminal cancer diagnosis. Unbeknownst to me, he made arrangements on a Saturday for his sister to fill the pool at her church and baptize me. I remember that day like it was yesterday. Daddy was so frail; half the size of the man he used to be. He was nothing like the man who used to haunt me. During my baptism, I hit the cold water and came up yelling, "JESUS!" Dad told my grandmother that he knew I had been touched. Afterwards, he gave me a look like the one Billy Dee Williams gave Diana Ross towards the end in the movie Mahogany after she found herself and that was the last time I saw my daddy.

At his wake, there were people from all walks of life and the church was packed. He knew how to make other people feel good. I guess that's where I get it from. I remember watching local drunks lining up and a lady saying, "Come on y'all we got to go see Tony." His obituary highlighted that his favorite scripture was Psalms 138:8, "The Lord will perfect that which concerns me; Your mercy, O Lord, endures forever; Do not forsake the works of Your hands."

I'm not sure what dad's issues were. I heard he wanted to go to college, but his dad wouldn't send him. His older brother was able to attend Xavier University and eventually became a pharmacist. Years later I visited his dad's house and found an old picture of my uncle, the pharmacist. I slid the back off the picture frame and found dad's high school report card. Mom claims he was very smart, but you could not tell by his grades. I'm uncertain whether granddaddy thought he didn't deserve the opportunity. I also don't know what impact the war had on my daddy. I often wonder what my life would have been like if I grew up with my father and mother in the same home.

Now that I know who I am in Christ, I forgive others and accept apologies that I never receive, especially from the man who God chose to be my earthly father. His seed of greatness has erupted in me to bring Him glory!

> *But I want you to know, brethren, that the things which happened to me have actually turned out for the furtherance of the gospel.*
>
> PHILIPPIANS 1:12

DON'T SWEAT THE SMALL STUFF... KEEP IT MOVING

ERIKA ZYNETTE GREENE

When I was younger, I would tell myself to laugh a lot, take risks, travel more and don't take myself too serious. The absolute best advice I can give you would be to seek God early for your purpose. Beware of people who will try to smother and dim your inner light. Most importantly, above all, forgive yourself, love yourself, live life to the fullest and never give up.

Please realize that some people come into your life for a season and some for a lifetime. Know the difference and do not devote too much time on seasonal people. Refuse to become a prisoner to the opinions of others. Be careful who you allow to speak into your life and strive to be the wonderful person God created you to be. Be yourself!

I always wanted to become a pediatrician but life threw me a curve ball. If for some reason you are unable to become what you thought you wanted to become--stay the course, keep the faith and never give up on yourself. Remember that God's plans are always better than what you could ever imagine. Save your money. Be wise with your spending for it will allow you to travel to exotic places and partake in exciting excursions.

Don't take yourself too seriously, loosen up. At times you can be your worst critic. So what you've made mistakes? Learn and grow from them, and keep it moving! Learn to love yourself unconditionally. You are beautiful, intelligent, smart, articulate and witty.

Forgive. Forgive. Forgive. You must refuse to succumb to the habit of not forgiving or harboring bitterness and resentment. Life is way too short. Let go of the hurt, disappointments and failures. It's all a part of life's process. Lastly, dream big--dream real big. Know beyond a shadow of doubt that God can dream bigger than you can dream for yourself. Enjoy your life's journey. Enjoy your life every single day!

Have dreams so big that it literally takes an act of God to achieve them.

UNKNOWN

BORN AGAIN

EVELYN GUINYARD

Nicodemus asked, "How can I reenter my mother's womb?" This question is the premise of the most important segment of my life. I was literally born again after years of negating God's love for me. The separation I felt from God and my rebirth were both affected by the deaths of people close to me.

February 9, 1959, my maternal grandmother passed. In my 10-year-old eyes, she was perfect. My brother and I would visit our grandparents each summer and on certain holidays. I remember sitting on her front porch listening to her sing and hum, "What a Friend We Have in Jesus," "The Old Rugged Cross," and "How I Got Over." Many summer evenings, Thomas and I rocked, listened and watched as cars drove by on the dusty red Georgia clay road in Washington, Georgia. Drivers always blew their horns and sometimes slowed down to speak. When people walked down my grandmother's street, they would say, "How you doing, Ms. Roberta?" "How is Mr. Robert doing?" and "Your flowers are so beautiful." A beautiful flower yard sat on the left side of the house. It was filled with all kinds of beautiful flowers, and my grandmother took care of them. I loved helping her in the yard.

Neighbors would often come by to ask if my grandparents needed any help. A few years before my grandmother's passing, she had a stroke and her left side became partially paralyzed. Nevertheless, she took care of her home, her blind husband, her flower yard and cared for us each summer. I tried to help her any way I could. I loved my grandparents so much.

In Atlanta on February 8, 1959, my mother rushed and prepared Thomas and I to go to my grandparents' house. When we arrived, we went in one at a time to say goodbye to my beloved grandmother. She passed! I couldn't understand why God would call her to be with Him. I thought,

"What about me, can I go too? If God loved us so much why would he take away the kindest, sweetest lady in the world? My mother said that Grandma was in a better place and we had to trust God. Over the next few months, I had many different thoughts about my grandmother. My prayer was for God to send her back to us. My mother and I were sad, and my brother would cry when he saw us cry. Was it my fault? Did I do something and God was punishing me by taking my grandmother? I decided that God was not lovable and mean. However, I didn't tell anyone how I felt. Throughout my childhood and teen years, I still attended Sunday school and Church, but in my heart, I just didn't believe God loved me.

One damp and dreary Sunday afternoon, two of my college classmates and I were traveling back to school from a weekend in Atlanta. At the time, I didn't know that death would play a pivotal role in my spiritual journey again. That afternoon, my friends and I were involved in a head-on collision with a man in a pickup truck. The impact threw me out of the car onto the shoulder. Both drivers were killed. I sustained a broken leg, broken arm, punctured lung, internal bleeding and many cuts and abrasions. The doctor told my family I may not make it through the surgery. I began to pray. This was my first sincere prayer since I was 10 years old. I thanked God for saving my life and asked Him to forgive my sins and protect me while I was in surgery. Unable to speak, I prayed in my heart and mind. I told God that I needed Him to help, and He did! I survived! That night in Crisp County Hospital, I was reborn. I became a new creature who loved God and knew that He loved me.

> *Therefore, if anyone is in Christ, he is a new creation; old things have passed away; behold, all things have become new.*
>
> 2 CORINTHIANS 5:17

FAITH MAKING WELL!

JOAN HARVEY HADLEY

Joan H. Hadley

"**G**od wants you to grow in grace, live by faith and walk by faith." ~ 2 Peter 3:18

When I was eight years old I was very ill and unable to walk. The doctors told my parents I was diagnosed with a disease that was only known in foreign countries. They also said that American doctors were in the process of looking for a cure. The disease attacked my spine. I was in and out of the hospital where doctors tested and completed spinal taps on my back. I missed many days of school in the 3rd grade. I will never forget my teacher, Mrs. Fannie Fambro. Back in the day, there was no such thing as homebound teachers. I am thankful for the times Mrs. Fambro came to my home and worked with me. I was unable to sit up most of the time. At the end of the school year, she explained to my parents she felt I would be able to catch up, so she promoted me to the fourth grade. Mrs. Hughes was my 4th grade teacher. She was aware of my condition and tutored me after school. My parents always prayed for my healing. Matthew 8:17 states, "He himself took our infirmities and bore our sicknesses."

Throughout the years, I was very successful in school. I graduated from Fort Valley State University with a bachelor's degree in Early Childhood Education and a master's degree from the University of Georgia.

Nurturing and supporting the growth of students fulfilled me. I taught elementary school for 31 years then retired. After retirement, I went back and worked for 11 more years. God gave me a gift to work with children by guiding and inspiring them to reach their potential.

God gave me a talent to do many things with excellence. I am grateful for being able to mentor young people. My purpose in life is to seek the will of God and to be a doer of God's Word. It is my hope and prayer that you will apply God's Word to your life. I pray that His Word will provide you with the divine capacity that impels you through the guidance of the Holy Spirit to serve the church, be loyal, give and help others.

In 2012, I went to the doctor for my six-month checkup and was advised to see a heart specialist. I was told I needed to have open heart surgery. I rebuked the diagnosis in the name of Jesus. The doctor asked me if I knew the seriousness of my condition. I told him, "I'll let you know," and went home and told my husband. The doctor called our home and told me that I needed to have surgery as soon as possible. I knew this was another storm, and I began to call on the name of Jesus. My prayer was Psalm 118:17, "I shall live and not die and declare the works of the Lord."

This year, 2015, I am testifying that I received a report on May 2015 stating that I am doing well! The doctor told me to continue believing. When I think of His goodness and all he has done for me throughout the years, I say thank you Lord! I know God healed me to do what I am destined to do and that is to serve others. Every day I bind my feet to the paths the Father has ordained for me to walk in. And I decree that my steps will be stronger and steady for I plead the blood of Jesus over me to help as I serve others daily.

I praise God for my spouse, Joe Hadley. If God is in the plan, you will have a strong marriage. You and your mate should always trust and believe in each other even when problems arise. My husband and I take out time to talk about our interests and activities. We enjoy putting time aside for each other. You and your mate must become one. I am thankful for my daughter Francenia who is a cancer survivor. I am also thankful for my grandchildren, Chardae and Isaiah and my great grandchildren, Nyelle, Jeremiah and Marcus.

I pray that your life will continue to reflect the greatness of God's blessings!

> *Trust in the Lord with all thine heart and lean not unto thy own understanding. In all thy ways acknowledge Him and he will direct your paths.*
>
> PROVERBS 3:5-6.

GRANDMOTHER'S LOVE LINGERS

JOE HADLEY, JR.

When I was a young child I didn't like to receive spankings from my mother. I really loved my grandmother, so I asked her if I could live with her? My father said it was okay.

I will never forget the time we went downtown Tallahassee to the Five and Dime store. While my grandmother was shopping, a lock attracted my attention. I liked the clicking and opening sound it made. Like grandmothers always do, she told me to put it back where I got it from. Needless to say, I didn't listen. She had no idea that I put the lock in my pocket. When I got home, I went out on the front porch and began playing with it. She overheard me playing and asked why I disobeyed her? She then, spanked me. That was the only time she ever spanked me. After the spanking, we walked back to the store and she made me apologize to the owner. Grandmother also asked him if I would be allowed to come to the store after school to work it off as punishment for my actions. Grandmother instilled important values in me because she loved me. Through all the ups and downs she faced, I saw a Godly and awesome woman. I always heard her pray at night. Her prayers and love made me a strong and hardworking man.

Grandmother always asked me if I completed my homework? Although she was unable to read, she would come in my room so I could show her my work.

My grandmother walked me 15 miles back and forth to school every day until the end of 9th grade. My fellow football teammates would tease me. At FAMU High School, I played as the quarterback during my junior and senior year.

After moving to Atlanta in 1965, I began to understand God's plans and purpose for me. For many years, as a football and basketball coach, I mentored young people. I still encourage my mentees to work smart, hold up the light and walk in the path of Jesus

I am married to the love of my life, Joan. When I met her she reminded me so much of my grandmother. She truly loves the Lord and lives by example.

> *Whoever does not love does not know God, because God is love.*
>
> 1 JOHN 4:8

GOD'S PLAN OF COMPASSION

SHIRLEY HAILE

Our legacy is defined as something we pass from one generation to the next. It is our distinctive contribution and commitment. I realized early on that God had a plan for my life. There are so many experiences I could share that influenced who I am today. But I will only talk about two of the experiences that happened very early in my life.

When I was 5 years old, my best friend contracted an incurable disease. My best friend, Mary Ann, was in a wheel chair. No one ever explained to me exactly what her condition was. I imagine it was cancer or something like that. She away when I was about 6 or 7. I haven't forgotten her. Her death profoundly impacted me.

Another friend of mine suffered serious burns when I was around 7 years old. I remember other children refused to play with her, because the dressing on her burned body "smelled funny." My great grandmother told me I have to overlook the smell in order to help Sandra heal and feel better. God instilled compassion in me at a very young age. I can't share it all, but many of my family members and friends influenced my life for the better. I can see God at every turn leading and guiding me.

Later in my adult life, my maternal grandmother became my hero. She was one of a kind. It is because of her that I live each day striving to make a difference. I make it a goal to touch peoples' lives. I plan to leave the world on a positive note, because I have lived.

I try to teach my children, my grandchildren, my friends and my peers to do all things with excellence. Granted, we all will make mistakes in life. We correct what we can and leave the rest to God and move forward. I taught my children proper work ethics. I worked for 47 years and retired in 2012. I firmly believe that knowing is not enough; we must apply. Willing is not enough; we must do.

My wish is for my children to eventually become entrepreneurs. My cousin called me a few

weeks ago and said he heard from our former schoolmate from elementary school, Ricky Ricks. When they talked, I was the first person Ricky asked about. I have not seen or heard from Ricky since third grade. My cousin said Ricky stated that, "Shirley was always so smart, and she helped me with my schoolwork." He said he never forgot me over these 60 years. That really made my day. I was pleased to hear that I had an impact on someone's life at such an early stage in life.

I am a mother of three children. Due to my divorce, I raised my children alone to the best of my ability. I tried to raise them in the fear and admonition of the Lord. I am thankful that they each know and love the Lord today. They strive to have peace with all men, and they willingly try to help people any way they can.

My grandchildren also fear and reverence the Lord. They are eager to reach out and help people. They love to do volunteer work with me. We are a very close family. This kind of legacy is worth more than silver and gold. To God be the glory for all He has done in me, through me and for my family.

> *Carve your name on hearts, not tombstones. A legacy is etched into the minds of others and the stories they share about you.*
>
> — SHANNON L. ALDER

WHEN MY FEET STOPPED WALKING, MY HEART STARTED TALKING

SHER HARRIS

I was born Sherion "Princess" Kidd on March 9, 1952, in Yazoo City, Mississippi, to Alex C. Hopson and Ester Lee Kidd. My parents, siblings and everyone in the neighborhood called me, "Kidd," "The chocolate brown love child," and "The spunky and feisty one." I have two sisters, two brothers and I am the eldest of five. My father sang in a gospel quartet when I was very young, and all the children were included in the group. My father didn't allow us to choose the genres we had to sing or play. I really couldn't hold a tune in a buckle compared to the other kids, so my dad assigned me the tambourine. I played it like nobody's business adding the moves and the rhythm. My mother lived in Chicago and was a member of a blues band with my uncle. I lived with mom during the school year and with dad during the summer. You could say I had the best of both worlds. My dad would call it, "straddling the fence between Heaven and Hell," and "playing the devil's music." My parents, as different as they were instilled strong morals and values in us that kept us in line. Church was always the center of our lives and the foundation of my personal development as a child. With my grandmother, "Big Mama," around, there was no, "spoil the child spare the rod." We got the rod, the hand, the switch and whatever else they could put their hands on. The golden rules in our household were respect and obedience. As I grew up I held those rules dear to my heart. I became a young, passionate woman about my family and those close to me. I cherish the good old days.

Well, I went on to marry my high school sweetheart. We were married for nearly 30 years and from that union, we had two beautiful children. We were a happy family with strong Christian values. During those years, I supported my husband with everything he did. My job was to work behind the scenes. I was a housewife his help-meet, best friend and proud of it. We worked together to build our American dream. He was our breadwinner, which gave me the opportunity to volunteer in the community. I served in PTA and many other volunteer groups. Years later, my dream life ended!

I was always a fashionista. For years I wore high heels no matter the circumstances. I even wore them when we moved from Chicago to Texas which is a totally different climate. I was even advised to change to flip flops or cowboy boots because of the terrain. My ankles took the blunt of it all. After several years, my feet became very weak and badly damaged. I endured a lot of pain and agony. Finally consulting a podiatrist, surgery was the only solution to relieve my pain. Little did I know, a change of shoes was a sign that my journey would change too. Per Bishop Dale C. Bronner, "God will let your feet start to hurt so you can change directions."

Once my feet stopped walking, my heart started talking and my legacy began. That's when God really grabbed my attention. He stopped me dead in my tracks and took me off my feet, literally. I was always moving and doing something for somebody. I always had something to do or somewhere to go. But I was missing the mark of what God wanted me to do. He wanted me to come from behind the scenes and heal His people. In other words, He put me on Front Street. Through my painful surgery and long recovery, God had my full attention. I couldn't go anywhere or do anything. I was in a wheelchair for several months and then to a walker. I was unable to take care of my four-year-old daughter, my son or my husband. For once, I had to focus on me. I needed someone to come take care of me. God showed me I wasn't in control, He was. I came clean with God. My conversation with Him was much needed and way overdue. It was necessary for me to go to the next level in life.

I was depressed and misplaced, my close friend convinced me to join her at an exercise class. I really didn't want to go. She said, "You need to get out of this house." Once we arrived at the class, I felt uncomfortable. I couldn't stand on my feet or participate. I was embarrassed being in class in a wheelchair. As I sat there in the back of the class watching the women work out feeling sorry for myself, God spoke to me. He said he wanted me to help His people and show them how to take care of themselves. I thought, "What… I can't even take care of myself!" As I sat there, He gave me a vision of how I could take this idea back to my community to help people regain their temple. It became clear to me what my mission and purpose was. I made a commitment to God, right then and there. If He would heal me and get me out of this wheelchair, I would do whatever he wanted me to do. My light bulb went off as I sat there watching the instructor dance to a Michael Jackson song. I always liked dancing, but never knew what to do with it. It took several months, but God healed me and eventually, I was able to participate in the exercise classes.

I moved from the back of the class to the front within a year. I went on to get certified through the I.D.E.A. the (International Dance Exercise Association) a couple years later and earned the chance to get on stage. Learning about health and fitness was a life saver. This holistic approach that came in the presence of God got me back to my roots and into Godly things. Health is life and good health is living. 3 John 1:2 states, "Beloved, I pray that in all respects you may prosper and be in good health, just as your soul prospers."

God healed my feet, heart and mindset for my journey. This desire to do God's will sent my marriage tumbling into divorce which sent my life into a tailspin. I tirelessly worked for years to help build my husband's business and my own. Success for one and failure for the other will upset even the best of marriages. However, I never gave up trying, working and pressing forward to make everything work out for everybody. I was determined to keep the peace, save our marriage, our family and keep our businesses going strong. After all was said and done, I was depressed. I suffered emotionally. I didn't know what to do, how to do it or which way to go. I was lost. My family was my world. I felt like a rock was dropped into the pond and the ripple effect sent us all in different directions. I no longer had my comfortable life surrounded by my children or my spouse.

My low self-esteem reared its ugly head. Due to my dark-colored skin, for years my sisters told me I shouldn't wear bright colors or stand in front of people. So, for a long time I dulled out and stood back. Now, God wanted me to motivate people. He knew He had to peel off the layers of doubt, self-shame and rebuild my confidence. He spoke to me thru a magazine one night, and told me to get up and get out from amongst them. I wrestled with this request, because I could not leave my children. They needed me. Yes, they were grown and started their own families, but in my heart I couldn't leave them. One day in the midst of the storm, I walked to the grocery store praying for directions. I was unemployed with no money and about to lose my house. My ex-husband drove by in some other woman's car laughing and having a good time. I realized that day I needed to leave and get away from the madness that became a lifestyle.

When I arrived in Georgia, I was depressed, downhearted and suicidal. I felt like a zombie walking around looking at happy couples laughing and enjoying life with their children. One morning a neighbor saw me sitting on my front porch and invited me to her church. The pastor asked, "Are you keeping the commitment you made to God when you were down and out? Are you doing what He asked you to do?" I fell on my face. I prayed for healing, purpose and a reason to live. It took several years for that healing to occur. In the meantime, I went back to what I knew, which was teaching fitness. I developed a program I could take to my new community. The program was doable for all and healthy safe and fun. God blessed me with a great job. It was my first real job and I am still there many years later. My first fitness location was at the senior center. For eight years, I taught weekly to seniors during my lunch hour. My business has grown by leaps and bounds since then. As my favorite scripture says, "I wish above all things that you prosper and be in good health." Health and wealth go hand in hand. You need good health to be able to achieve wealth, and you need good mental health to be able to enjoy it. We can defeat bad health and bad habits. We need to really look at what we have done to ourselves, what side effects we have developed and then get in the business of reversing what we've done. It is not too late, it just demands commitment.

When my health began failing, it dawned on me that my life changed and would never be the same. I learned three important lessons. I allowed depression to set in and negatively affect my health. Once depression overcame me, I was almost convinced that my life was over and worthless. Satan attacked my mind and robbed me of my health. I became self-destructive. For several months I lived in one room. I often laid in a fetal position crying about my loss. God sent my neighbor over to rescue me and minister to me. She reminded me what He called me to do.

The second lesson I learned was about the empowerment I gained from my experiences. I was ashamed to share my life with anyone. I never allowed my true feelings to show on the outside, because I didn't want anyone's pity or handout. I was engaged in the things of God, serving him by helping His people take care of their health through proper nutrition and exercise. Earlier years in my life I was so focused on taking care of others, I neglected the temple God gave me. I was too busy to take care of myself. I searched deeper inside myself to find that voice that was muzzled for so long. I cried out to God, and He heard my cry. My voice mattered. Did you know that your journey will introduce you to yourself? It will expose the champion that lives inside of you. God will cause an earthquake to shake up your life so that you can be directed to the path He destined for your life. No matter what or where you came from, God will give you the strength to complete the journey He declared for you.

Thirdly, because I grew up around music, it was easier for me to stand before an audience and talk about health, fitness, praise, and healthy eating habits. God prepared me with the music of dance in my soul and a gift of gab. The Holy Spirit exposed me so I could live out the destiny inside of me. God awakened me so I could leave the appropriate legacy. Many people ask me today, "How have you managed all these years?" I don't know. All I know is that He would not let me rest until I delivered the message He placed in my heart.

I received my life's lessons well. As Bishop Dale C. Bronner said, "The world is a book and he who does not travel only reads one page." You have to know when it's time to turn the page. I learned this lesson on my journey. God has allowed my journey to be very rewarding and exciting. God will make your latter days rich and fruitful beyond measure. Mental illness is not forever. With time, effort and God, it shall pass. God healed my broken heart, mind and body.

He has set my feet on a path that glorifies Him in everything I do. Every time I see someone's life transform by eating healthier, exercising and working to stay in shape, I am encouraged to, "keep on keeping on." I know in my heart I would not have made it this far without God. Today I am stronger, wiser and better because of God's presence in my life. To God be all the Glory! And may you leave a legacy of never giving up too!

> *When you get into a tight place and everything goes against you, till it seems as though you could not hang on a minute longer, never give up then, for that is just the place and time that the tide will turn.*
>
> HARRIET BEECHER STOWE

THE STORY OF TEDDY BEAR

REV. CAROLYN HANKS HOLLEY

In 1990, I felt like a lonely and rejected Teddy Bear. So, I wrote, "Teddy Bear," a poetic story about a teddy bear that was given to me at a fair in 1959. Instead of being thrown away, teddy bears and other stuffed animals can be washed. Jesus Christ's human teddy bears can also be washed. We shouldn't throw them away. We should show God that we truly love Him by caring for His special creations.

The Lord is calling for us to reason with Him. He is softly and tenderly urging us to plant a divine spirit-filled garden. We must fertilize this garden with the Holy Ghost. Let us be aware that the devil does not want us to plant this garden. As we cultivate our garden, we must wear the whole armor of God. The Holy Spirit will lead us to plant a row of love, joy, peace, long suffering, gentleness, goodness, faith, meekness and temperance. As we gather the fruits, let us not forget to save healthy seeds to replant our gardens. Let's share our fruits and seeds with all precious Teddy Bears.

Jesus is warning us with loving care to share love and salvation everywhere! When I was a sweet-16 beautiful teenage queen, there were things I wished for that seemed like a dream. I owned some dolls and a few other toys, but never owned a teddy bear and would always spot them at the fair. The fair was located right in front of our house and we'd sneak in through the cracks like little measly mice. The workers didn't care and pretended they didn't see us. They knew we didn't have money. One night, I teasingly told one of the workers in great despair, "You have so many Teddy Bears, you wouldn't miss him. Please give me the one over there." The worker exclaimed, "No! No! My child I can't do such a thing! I must obey my boss! For in this show, he is the king." So, I sadly smiled and walked away. But, each night I would pay the teddy bear stand a visit.

On the last night of the fair I wouldn't go near the bears. I knew I would break down and cry and have to tell the teddy bears goodbye. Then, I heard a loud and clear voice, "Young lady, please come over here." I quickly ran to the teddy bear stand and the man placed the loveliest teddy bear in my hand. He told me, "He's yours for keeps." I was so happy I began to weep, and I kindly and humbly thanked him. I promised to love and care for Teddy each day. After receiving my gift, I ran as fast as a pistol shot to the photographer's spot. I hopped on the stool and proudly kissed Teddy Bear right on his black nose. I pinched myself. My mind was in a whirl. Yes! I was the happiest teenage girl in the world.

Teddy and I had so much fun. There were times when we would play until the day was done. When I was lonely and sad, I would hold him tightly and sleep so peacefully throughout the night. When my sister Fran came home for the holiday, she hugged sweet Teddy in a special way. When it was time for her to leave, she begged to take Teddy and said, "Don't say no."

Of course I didn't want to let Teddy go, but Fran was my only sister. Heaven knows I loved her. She was doing so well in college. She earned good grades and obtained great knowledge. It was a sad decision for me, but I wanted Fran to be happy. In a bittersweet tone I said, "With you, Teddy I will share, if you promise to give him genuine love and care." I graciously explained that Teddy Bear was so special to me, and without him, I would experience much misery. "So Fran, take care of him and bring him back. Agree?" She agreed and off to school they went. I missed my Teddy and I spent many lonely nights waiting for the school year to be over. I knew she was bringing Teddy back beyond any doubt.

Around June 1, Fran arrived home on a sunny afternoon. I happily asked, "Where's Teddy Bear?" Fran looked at me with a glimpse of despair, "Carol, I don't have him, I'm sorry to say Teddy got dirty, and I threw him away." I exclaimed, "Oh no! No! Fran, I don't understand. An act like that was not in the plan, you promised as one would on a witness stand to love and take care of Teddy, you see, you promised and I trusted you to bring him back to me."

In heaven, I'll search for my Teddy Bear. My love for him is still the same. The only way to ease this childish pain is for me to have him again. Teddy Bear, are you there in the land so bright and fair? Has Jesus cleaned and washed you up and sat you in a golden chair? Sister Fran, please meet me there. For you, I still love and care. And should I find my Teddy Bear, he will still be ours to share. In the name of Jesus, let's work toward collecting Jesus Christ's Human Teddy Bears right here on earth. Should they be soiled from natural dirt or soiled from the stain of hurt, failure, loneliness, sickness, pain, poverty or whatever. In the name of Jesus, let's wash them up, fluff them up and brush their tangled hair, and sit them oh so proudly in a very special chair.

We're doing better about being readers and hearers of the Word. Now, let's get down to the real thing and become great spirit-filled doers of the Word, and Jesus will keep washing us up, brushing us up and untangling our entangled hair and sit us oh so proudly one day in an eternal golden chair.

And now why are you waiting? Arise and be baptized and wash away your sins calling on the name of the Lord.

ACTS 22:16

FOR A GIVING – NOT FOR A LIVING

GILBERT HUNTER

I am a "Grady Baby," but my parents moved to Buffalo, New York, when I was a child. At age 18, I joined the Army. My dad encouraged me to get a career not a job, so I was determined to make a career out of the military. I stayed in there until I turned 39. I started in the Army Airborne division and was sent to Jump School. I retired with full benefits. While in the Army, I served during the Vietnam War. War is something you never get over and it tests your faith, belief and reliance upon the Almighty One – Jesus Christ. I still deal with trauma from the war, but my faith and my giving keeps me going strong.

Towards retirement, I was assigned to the Ranger Division and served as an instructor. Ranger training is a type of training that will test a person's endurance. As an instructor, we were taught to break a person down and rebuild them to a higher level. The purpose was to ensure soldiers stayed strong during combat. After the military, I worked a special Army detail for an independent military contractor. I was a part of a special elite training force. My assignment was in Saudi Arabia. I had the duty of training the body guards of Saudi Arabia's King Fahd. That assignment lasted two years.

When the assignment ended, I moved back to Georgia and began working with the United States Postal Service. Throughout the years I've dabbled with photography. I always enjoyed taking pictures of people and giving them back their prints. Since I was getting retirement pay from the Army and earning decent money with the Post Office, I really didn't need anything. I received more enjoyment out of seeing my customer's reactions when they viewed their prints.

When I moved back to Atlanta, I started going to Rev. Charles Stanley's church and eventually found my way to Word of Faith (WOF) at the East Point, Georgia, location. I saw Bishop on television, visited the church and been there ever since. I found the people at WOF to be warm and welcoming. After a year, I joined WOF. My membership number is 303. I began taking pictures and giving them to the congregation. I get a joy out of giving. I am blessed to be a blessing. To this day, I still take pictures and have taken pictures for Bishop and his family. God has been good to me. I retired from two careers. Now, I'm able to do what I love to do. I do it, not for the money, but for the joy of giving to others.

In closing, I'm reminded when God asked Moses, "What's in your hands?" Throughout the years I have held a camera in my hands amidst my careers and living. It has always given me a sense of purpose and joy. I show God's love to others by capturing moments of their life. How do you show God's love to others? Don't be afraid to share your gifts, talents and abilities with others. When you give, you receive a priceless reward.

> *Blessed are those who give without remembering and take without forgetting.*
>
> ELIZABETH BIBESCO

MISSIONARY NURSE ON A MISSION

SHIRLEY A. HUNTER

When my father passed, I was only a few months old. I was told that I was his pride and joy. As I became older my mother began to work many hours to provide, so my two older brothers and our neighbors cared for us. My mom eventually remarried a man by the name of Howard Stafford and moved the family to West Virginia. He was a very mean man but made lots of money and was a big church tither. In our new home in West Virginia, we lived in a very nice community of both blacks and whites. Our neighborhood was very close and families helped care for each other's children. We were a close knit community that felt more like an extended family.

At the age of 16 I married a man named Robert. I was the youngest in the neighborhood to marry, but at that point I felt that my mother no longer wanted me in the house and my relationship with my step-father was failing. I still remember being extremely nervous on my wedding day. I asked the pastor which side should I stand on and he replied "It doesn't matter; you're breaking your neck anyway." At the time, I didn't understand what that meant but soon learned when the challenges of being a teenage wife began to surface.

I tried to continue school, but the babies were coming and my mother said she no longer had the energy to help me. In an effort to be a good wife, I dropped out of school. My parents moved out from under us and moved into their own home. I missed my mother. I remember the times we spent on the front porch drinking RC Cola, eating peanut butter crackers and swinging on cool summer evenings. Well, I was married now and had to grow up and it wasn't a bed of roses. After a few years of marriage I decided to go to school. The children were older so I felt it was a good time to try again. I always wanted to be a nurse so I finished high school then went off to college for my nursing degree.

I worked really hard and continued going to college while working two and three jobs. I worked private duty cases, worked as a labor and delivery nurse, a charge nurse supervisor and an instructor. I worked so hard my husband would bring me fresh uniforms to the hospital. I had no time for anything but work. Even though I worked, I learned that a good nurse always takes a lunch and a vacation.

Although I enjoyed the field of nursing, something was missing. My schedule was very conflicting so I searched for a nearby Baptist church I could attend that would fit into my schedule. However, I failed to find one. One day I was told, "Well, there is a white boy in Edison who is really bringing in the souls." My reply was, "Well, you know I don't like White preaching." He replied, "Well there is Rev. L. on Central Ave."

So, I visited that church one night. It was a beautiful church, but they were in the basement that night. Low and behold, the preacher was a woman. I started talking to my Lord, "Lord you know I don't like women preachers." Before I knew it, I was at the altar on the floor. The Lord said, "I got what you need." The message was powerful! I began speaking in tongue. The Holy Spirit was in the room. But, Satan was not about to let me go that easy.

My journey as a nurse continued. I went from a bedside nurse to becoming a nurse in foreign countries where communists would chase us. Our lives were routinely threatened, however, we knew we were safe because we were doing God's will. As a registered nurse and missionary, prayer is a must.

I traveled to Suarez, Mexico, where the people raise their family in garbage dumps and would deliver their babies there too. People would look for cardboard boxes to sell for 25 cents each. The fathers stood in lines for boxes of cereal and winter coats. The wealthier people would bring half a sandwich from their lunch and share with others. This experience really made you thankful for what you have.

We held church at night to talk about Christ. Many of the gang members were converted. They let us know by turning their caps around. Many souls received the Holy Spirit.

We went from camp to camp casting out devils and laying hands on the sick. We donated over 200 pounds of food that included rice, macaroni, sugar, and lots of other food. Evangelizing is rewarding when you think about the goodness of Jesus and all that he has done for us. My journey in life has prepared me to be a better servant for the Lord. Instead of complaining about my struggles and my past I, just say. "Thank you Jesus because it could have been worse."

Count your blessings instead of your crosses;
Count your gains instead of your losses.
Count your joys instead of your woes;
Count your friends instead of your foes.
Count your smiles instead of your tears;
Count your courage instead of your fears.
Count your full years instead of your lean;
Count your kind deeds instead of your mean.
Count your health instead of your wealth;
Count on God instead of yourself.

UNKNOWN

DO NOT ALLOW YOUR EMOTION TO RUN OR RULE YOUR LIFE

SHIRLEY L. IGBERAESE

A life lesson that I'd like to share: Ladies, and especially young ladies, do not allow your emotions to run or rule your life. As soon as you truthfully recognize this foe in your life (do not deceive yourself or lie to yourself), begin to pray and seek Jesus with your soul, heart, and hands wide open. Do not walk or skip, but run to Jesus, and begin to pray for understanding, knowledge, and wisdom, to overcome the floods of emotions we wade through as women. Thank God for the waves that brings joy, love and happiness. But give Jesus the burden to carry the things that drain, rob, and steal your joy from being who you truly are.

Shirley L. Igberaese

Beloved, do not be deceived, do not try to stand alone in seeking to overcome the flood of the ever-changing tides of emotions. Seek and ask for prayer from your pastor, prayer partner, and inner circle of friends. Surround yourself with saints when this foe attacks you as you walk through this earthly journey. You must have a made up mind to stand in Christ against the waves of your emotions. Stop and pray, if you do not have the gift to speak in tongues, stop, right now and invite the Holy Spirit to come into your heart, there is supernatural power in this gift. Take a stand. Always seek to please God, pray for guidance and then be still and listen. Try and walk in who Christ has anointed you to be. Emotions can and will invite fear to attack you if you do not a stand in Christ.

Know, receive, and believe Him. Our physical body was not built or designed to be withered or be weighed down with the changing tides of our emotions. In my past I experienced a lot of ups and downs, and my moods did not help either. These emotions can and will steal your health; my health was attacked. You will allow a door to open that will attack different parts of your body if you do not vigilantly stand in Christ. I am still here, because of love, favor, grace and mercy. Beloved, do not let the enemy trick you into following your tides of negative emotions, because God wants you to use wisdom. Wisdom says: "Wait a minute until the emotions settle down." It is very important to establish your walk in and with Christ on what you believe in His Word, instead of how you behave or feel. This directs your waves of emotions to disturb your journey in life. It is not a matter of merely being positive in order to change people or things around you, because you cannot; only Jesus and prayer can. Take a stand. It's a matter of believing the truth about who you are in Christ, not your emotions. And that's in the Word of God.

Beloved, in Christ, make emotional maturity a priority in your life. As women, we are passing on a powerful legacy to our daughters, granddaughters, and great grandchildren. We are teaching them how to be overcomers through our living and especially how we handle our emotions.

> *Therefore, my beloved brethren, be steadfast, immovable, always abounding in the work of the Lord, knowing that your labor is not in vain in the Lord.*
>
> 1 CORINTHIANS 15:58

GREEN MEANS GO

FLORENCE A. JACKSON

When the light is green, I go. The first green light I smoothly rode through was on March 4, 1933. On that day, I was born in Locust Grove, Georgia. The No. 1 song that day was, "Stormy Weather (Keeps Rainin' All the Time)," by Ethel Waters. It was funny, because it was not stormy that day; it was a dry 54 degrees. The No. 1 movie that day was, "King Kong." I wonder if my birth was caused that day because she was startled. Back then, it only cost about 35 cents to go to the movies. I was the 11th of 12 children born to my parents. Being the last daughter had its advantages, but it also had its disadvantages such as picking cotton, milking cows and doing general farm work. Farm life was all I knew, aside from church and school. I was baptized in a creek in Shiloh and attended Shiloh Elementary in Jenkinsburg, Georgia.

My next green light appeared when I was in the 7th grade. I moved to Atlanta to live with my sister and grandmother. This was a huge change from farm living, but I was able to adapt and continue thriving. I faithfully attended Whites Chapel after moving to the big city. I received my education from the public school system. I was a student at Howard Middle School which later became Howard High

School. I participated in the track and field as a high jumper, played basketball and was a member of the dance team. Here is an interesting little known fact about me, I played the violin. I could have been the female, "Stuff Smith," but God had other plans for me.

Upon graduating from high school, I planned to attend Tuskegee Institute to major in Alterations and Design. But the light was not green in that direction due to funding for material. So, instead I found that I could turn right on red and change my major to Health and Physical Education. While at Tuskegee, I met James Edward Jackson who became my husband. Graduating with a degree in Health and Physical Education, I moved to Florida to work at Dillard High School for two years. I got married on February 2, 1959, and became Annie Florence Gordon Jackson. On June 27, 1960, my greatest accomplishments were born: Dwayne Edward and Karen Denise Jackson.

Stoplights come in three different colors. Sometimes they are red which means stop. Sometimes they are yellow which means be very cautious, and sometimes they are green which means go. I was on go when I relocated to Atlanta. I taught at Turner High School for several years. Seeking to further my education, I enrolled in Ithaca College in Ithaca, New York, where I received a Master's Degree in Physical Education and General Science. I returned to Atlanta where I taught Physical Education at Southwest High School and retired from Benjamin E. Mays High School.

I have been honored with numerous green lights in life that had directional arrows. Some lights are red with green right arrows, but some are green with red right arrows. These are times in my life when I had to look through the peephole of life at knocking opportunities. An example was my chance to attend Jackson & Gates Dance School. It was located at the Waluhaje Hotel Apartment, a place that was popular for its ballroom that featured top jazz talents. Another arrow took me into the world of cosmetics where I became a consultant for Fashion 220 Cosmetics. Another arrow led me to start VIP Travel which afforded me to do something I love, travel. I have traveled to Alaska, Jamaica, Hawaii and Argentina just to name a few.

Following the green light I enjoyed the birth of my beautiful granddaughter. I was able to watch her grow from an infant to an adult. Over the years, I've opened my home and heart to numerous college students from Clark Atlanta University and Morehouse College. I have been a caretaker for my parents, sisters, nieces and nephews with no regrets.

So I sum up my life with 1 Corinthians 13:4-8; "Love is patient, love is kind. It does not envy, it does not boast, it is not proud. It is not rude, it is not self-seeking, it is not easily angered, it keeps no record of wrongs. Love does not delight in evil but rejoices with the truth. It always protects, always trusts, always hopes, and always perseveres. Love never fails." Sometimes a light may be red and if it is then make a right turn and continue driving. That is just like life, some may see a red light and stop, but for those who know better, even a red light can be a GO for a right turn.

> *If one advances confidently in the direction of one's dreams, and endeavors to live the life which one has imagined, one will meet with a success unexpected in common hours.*
>
> HENRY DAVID THOREAU

SET APART FOR GOD'S PURPOSE

CHARLES JOHNSON

Jeremiah. 1:5 states, "Before I formed you in the womb, I knew you, before you were born, I set you apart…"Always remember that you are set apart for God's purpose.

As I reflect on growing up in the backwoods of Bumpass, Virginia, I often think how God protected and directed me even when I rebelled against Him. I was raised by church-going, foster grandparents whose main desire for me was to stay out of trouble and graduate high school. I studied just enough and took just enough courses to graduate. I had no desire for higher education, but that wasn't God's plan for me.

As a small boy, I recall being on the verge of a copperhead snake bite. My grandfather was in the right place and time to kill it. Another time when a truck was backing into a building column, he was there to jerk me away from it falling on my head. There were times when God closed doors that prevented me from getting involved in things that would've been destructive for me. I didn't understand at the time that it was God's hand of protection and direction that often saved me. I'll begin in Atlantic City, New Jersey, summer of 1955. Each year, my high school's assistant principal would take a group of youth there to work for the summer. One evening, I stopped at a small storefront church filled with Blacks. The speaker was using everyone's last name and relating it to someone famous, and white of course. When I gave him my name, Johnson, he said, "You're probably related to Johnson & Johnson, have they ever did anything for you?" As I think back, I believe that he was the beginning of the Malcolm X movement.

I attended a segregated high school for the entire county of Louisa, Virginia. My graduating class of 1956 totaled 47 students. Upon graduation,

I located to Washington, DC, and got a job with the Marriott Corporation, which was then called Hot Shoppes. They operated family restaurants, government and business' cafeterias and two motor hotels. I held various positions at their distribution warehouse. The headquarters was located on the same site.

In 1958, the printmaker and office assistant in the Architectural and Engineering Office was promoted to draftsman. He suggested me as his replacement. However, I didn't know what a draftsman did. During my spare time, I traced over old dull and torn drawings, so I could learn how to use the tools for architectural lettering. After a while, I was promoted to draftsman and responsible for developing working documents from the rough sketches created by the architects and engineers. In 1961, I prepared to be drafted into the Army, so I enlisted into the Air Force where I spent eight years. I had a choice of going to a technical school or taking a bypass test for drafting. I only knew how to use the tools, so I failed the test and ended up in the motor pool as a vehicle operator and finally as a Quality Assurance Specialist for surface transportation. Much of my time was spent on loan to other departments as a draftsman. In 1965, when I was alerted for an assignment in Vietnam, I was married and my wife and I were expecting our youngest daughter. Again, I had a choice of reenlisting and going to Vietnam or resigning so I chose the latter – which was God's direction.

The transition program with the Air Force Separations Office arranged for me to go to a local technical school for a course in drafting as part of my duty day. Upon completion, I went on interviews, but I didn't qualify for any openings. So, I didn't know what was in store for me as a civilian. When the separations department contacted me, I considered employment other than drafting. They asked if I was interested in interviewing with Johnson & Johnson for a drafting position. Of course, I jumped at the opportunity. At my interview with my sponsor and the chief engineer, I presented my work from the technical school. The chief engineer said, "That's not what we're looking for, we need someone to do Architectural and Mechanical drafting." My heart leaped as I replied, "That's what I did for Marriott." I suppose they contacted Marriott, and my sponsor called me with an offer beyond what I expected. I was assigned to report to a project. A man named Ed Suliga, told me if I allowed him, he would help me move up the ladder. When I messed up, he would come down hard and when he finished, he would say, "Peace," and that was the end of it. He would tell me that the only place to find sympathy was in the dictionary. I nicknamed him, "my Polish Godfather." The director of engineering pushed me to enroll in college to the point of telling me that if I enrolled in college, he would make sure I had the money. I enrolled in an Architectural Technology course at a county college and subsequently an industrial engineering major at The College of New Jersey. I graduated the same year my daughter graduated from high school. Johnson & Johnson purchased a company that manufactured dental restoration products and rented a facility to house the newly formed Johnson & Johnson Dental Products Company. Ed was assigned to retrofit the facility, so we moved into that facility and handled the engineering work. Eventually, the company consisted of three facilities in the same industrial park. Ed was called to oversee a major corporate project. The dental company needed a project engineer, so he recommended me. At that time, I had less than two years of community college. One of the products was losing money so corporate decided to sell the company. A few months prior, the engineering director of Ortho Pharmaceutical Corp (J & J subsidiary) inquired to see if I was available to transfer to his staff. He was told that I wasn't available. So when the dental company started to reduce its staff on a Friday, it only took one phone call. I interviewed with Ortho on Monday and the director started me on a project that afternoon through a consignment agreement with the dental company. Within a few weeks, he posted a position that matched all of my experience and I was hired permanently as a construction project engineer. There were times when I messed up, but God's mercy kept me employed. I took a retirement buy-out from Ortho at the age of 55. Even before I knew God's direction, I always said I wanted to retire when I turned 55.

I tell this story, because I know God has directed every step of my career. Even when I regretted my early retirement, He directed me to where I am now. If I was in corporate America in the past, I don't believe I would have heard Him to make the decision to locate to Metro Atlanta. In summary: 1955: Atlantic City, New Jersey, man prophesies about Johnson & Johnson; 1956: employed by Hot Shoppes where I became a draftsman; 1965: leave military, attended free technical school and employed by Johnson & Johnson (all arranged by the military). My career was a divine set up. God had me where I needed to be in order to earn my degree and secure my career. My blessings outweigh my struggles.

God has also directed my spiritual life. In the late 70s, my family joined a church in New Jersey . We were having marital issues and considering divorce. I remember the pastor stating, "I don't believe in divorce, but this has been going on for too long." We were in the process of obtaining lawyers when our pastor met with us. He asked us to hold on for a couple of weeks until the annual revival because a couple was scheduled to minister on marriage. He told them about us and they scheduled an appointment with us. During that meeting, they showed us that our problem was satan seeking to destroy my family. We also got saved, and I was slain in the spirit to the point of speaking in tongues. I was told that they were unable to, "shut me up" until the Holy Spirit finished with me. God sent the right people at the eleventh hour to rescue my family. I won't claim that everything was smooth sailing for us after that, but through God we were able to weather each storm. He is faithful.

Even with my wife's death, I believe it was God's mercy. She spent months in hospitals and nursing homes. She was about to become an amputee which would have required more time in a rehab facility, which she dreaded. God took her home just days before her scheduled surgery. I believe she knew she was going by the conversation she had with our daughter just a couple of days prior to her death. I thank God that he prepared us to release her. I've said many times that if I had the opportunity to live my life over knowing what I know now, I would do many things differently. I'm sure we all would, but God had me all along.

For we are His workmanship, created in Christ Jesus for good works, which God prepared beforehand that we should walk in them.

EPHESIANS 2:10

WHY I DON'T HIT ROCK BOTTOM

LEANORIA JOHNSON

When I am unemployed or underemployed, I don't hit rock bottom. I remember times when not having a job initially caused me to experience fear. Each time I had to remind myself that I can do all things with the help of God. And God and I are co-creators of my destiny. These affirmations helped me to calm down during times of being unemployed and underemployed.

My lifestyle is soaking up the Word of God. When financial issues arise, I go deeper with scripture and meditation. I use savings and retirement money to keep "giving tithes" and maintain my lifestyle. God gave me good health, a sound mind, and the power to get wealth. He also gave me skills and talents to work and make money.

I budget and expand my money by writing down my spending. Also, I expand my money by buying opportunities that will make me more money. I hedge money to make sure that it is not wasted nor spent impulsively.

Regardless of your situation, creditors still want their payments. Some creditors offer forbearance programs. And some creditors offer hardship programs by accepting reduced payments. But these programs last for a limited time

I am experiencing no job security as I write this book submission. I finally realize that I want wealth security more than I want job security. I am carefully structuring my "time currency" and designing the life I really want. Now that I am seasoned and full of wisdom, my preference is to work on building my wealth security during productive hours. Building my wealth security assures me that I will not ROOM (Run Out of Money).

Whenever I am threaten with not generating income, it has been a temporary situation because I get up and do something about my life and my financial well-being.

During times of employment, I save money, purchase grams of gold, and deposit money into

cash investments. These are my safety nets when I am unemployed. You can do something about your financial stability, too. The sooner you choose wealth security over job security the better. First put most of your energy on the passionate work that builds wealth security. Second, work on a job to pay only necessary bills. It is like working two shifts. The most productive hours are for your wealth building events and the dead non-productive hours are for the job that pays only necessary bills. It is my hope that I eventually will be overflowing with wealth and cash flow.

As a seasoned Saint, I know now to put more focus on building generational wealth and leaving a legacy. I know now how important is to not leave bad debt that will burden my husband and our children. As for a job, I know now not to go for a job just for high pay. My passion for the job is just as important as the high pay. Having passion for my job helps me to stay when the going gets tough. I choose to be tough because I know that tough times don't last but tough people do.

I have shared some jewels. I invite you to write your vision and make it plain. Implement an action plan to make sure that you secure your prosperity "EARLY" in life. Finish your race regardless of the obstacles that may come your way. Take responsibility for your choices and take some risks in life to get something you've never had. If something goes wrong, there is a scripture that says this too shall pass. If you get hurt, there is a song that says pray until He heals the hurt. Be encouraged and remember that God has a good plan for your future. Bank on that.

> *If they obey and serve Him, they shall spend their days in prosperity, and their years in pleasures.."*
>
> JOB 36:11

KEEP YOUR SPIRITUAL VEHICLE MOVING-BRAKES ARE PROHIBITED

NATHANIEL JOHNSON

Mason, Tennessee, is a small town with only one traffic light. I was born on a farm in a wood-framed house whose foundation was anchored by tree stumps. My grandmother's sister was a midwife. I remember her going over the hills carrying a black leather bag as she performed her midwifery services of delivering babies in our community. Back then, your neighbor's house was quite a distance because of the land that farmers used to grow their crops. So, some days she had quite a commute to get to her patients who were joyfully waiting for the arrival of the next addition to their family. We owned only one pair of shoes which were to be worn only on Sundays at church. I can only imagine the countless number of miles she traveled barefoot throughout the community.

One day, when I was five years old, I was out in the field chopping cotton that granddaddy assigned to us kids. It was a very hot and sunny day, so we had a custom to bury our water bottles in the ground to keep them cool. We drew our water from the well, but it was just like water you would get out of a fridge. During the morning hour, the ground was still damp on the surface. After placing the water bottles in the hole, we used a twig to mark where we buried them. Suddenly, we noticed a dog with rabies approaching us. With a loud shout, one of the family members yelled out, "Run, don't let that dog bite you, he has distemper!" I believe distemper is what we call rabies today. He chased us all the way back to the farm house, and that wasn't nice at all. Then, he had a field party chasing the farm animals. Feathers were flying everywhere. The ducks, chickens, guinea hens and roosters were airborne, completely off the ground. Now, here is what happened. We had about seven hunting dogs which were away from the farm with other family members. When they heard the commotion, they stormed to the house to defend their territory, so the mad dog ran under the house and found the point where the bottom of the house was almost touching the ground.

We had work to do and this mad dog had gotten in our way. My uncle spoke out and said, "Go get the rifle," which he kept over the door in a rack. Because I was young and curious, I became excited about what to do in such an incident. My uncle laid on his belly and aimed at the dog that hid in a tight spot under the house. The shot rang out. Now, the question was how were they going to get the dog from under the house that was now located in the tight spot? All eyes beamed on me. I was given the rope and instructions to place the rope around the dog's elbows (not his neck). My assignment was quite treacherous; the location was slimy and tight. I had to crawl through the areas where the animals stayed overnight. The smell was extremely unpleasant. I finally reached him and placed the rope as instructed.

As I was crawling back from under the house, my britches got caught by a nail. The men were not paying me that much attention after they knew I roped the dog. I decided to slide sideways where the ground was lower. Finally, when I was completely out from under the house, we took the dog across the road and threw it in the gully and went back to work.

On the following day we were back at work at the same field that needed finishing. Granddad had another field waiting on us. We got our water bottles and buried them. As I was chopping away, I looked up and spotted the same dog we encountered the day before. I noticed the mark from the bullet over his left eye. We were shocked the dog wasn't dead. We threw large clogs of dirt, and one of them hit him in his side. It must have hurt, which made him think about what happened to him the day before. You can only imagine how I felt knowing that the dog wasn't dead. He could have eaten me up under that house and nobody would have been able to reach me. Many times, I look back over my life and know that God, and only GOD, can work a miracle to shut down a mad animal so that I can do a job that nobody else could have done.

Many years after that life-changing experience, I witnessed and was the recipient of life-changing moments that began in 1965 at Bronner Brothers Enterprise located at Hunter and Ashby Streets in Atlanta, Georgia. This location is now MLK Drive. I was a hungry, seeking and motivated student seeking knowledge on how to become a successful entrepreneur. That platform was produced by Mr. Nathaniel Bronner and his brother Arthur Bronner. Mr. Nathaniel Bronner was a man of integrity and a light in the community. He always wore a smile and greeted everyone with love and kindness. He wore a suit and tie every day and drove a green Volkswagen van. He would always let you know that it was not about him, but he always wanted to know how he could help you. His example planted seeds in me that taught me to never give up, keep pushing until I reach my goal.

There are two days that are important to each of us: the day you enter the earth and the day you embrace the reason you were born. When we discover our reason, it directly connects us to our Father that gave us life and purpose for being on earth. God saved me years ago at a very young age. And to this day – He remains by my side. After being on this planet for a few years – here's a few words to ponder.

- Read books about what you are interested in
- Study people who are doing what you want to do
- Pay God first, yourself second and your bills last
- Share your love and love everybody
- Let your actions speak louder than your words
- Start early in figuring out what you want to do
- Learn your history

THE SIGNIFICANCE OF MENTORSHIP

WILLIAM LEE JOHNSON, JR

I want to share a life lesson about the significance of mentorship when fulfilling your dreams and aspirations. It takes God's grace to face your fears of discrimination and humiliation. I grew up in South Carolina where I was the first to integrate my local high school. This presented many challenges of overcoming stereotypes. Despite the name calling and discouragement, I never lost sight of completing high school and college.

While in high school, I struggled with mathematics and science. I did not understand the significance of having good study habits and taking advantage of tutors. In addition, I couldn't rely on my father, because he only had a 9th grade education. My fellow classmates thought I was too dumb to learn anything. I was the focus of their bullying and jokes. In spite of the negative criticism from my peers, I kept pressing forward. I attended summer school for three years of high school. When I graduated from high school, my grades were not stellar and my parents could not afford to send me to college. I entered a technical school to take up a trade. I did not want to work in the cotton mill like some of my classmates. However, after my high school graduation, I ended up working at the cotton mill. The experience convinced me to look for other alternatives. One of my former co-workers from the cotton mill asked me, "Are you coming back to work with us?" I replied, "Not if I can help it and I will never look back." The cotton mill was a great motivator to seek a better life for myself.

After working in the cotton mill, I set my sights on learning a trade. I watched my father wire electrical boxes and do plumbing; I became fascinated with electronic gadgets including television and radios. I pursued a trade at Masse Technical Institute in Jacksonville, Florida. The journey at Masse Technical Institute was a different environment. There was no bullying or people telling rude jokes. This was a great relief. For the first time I understood the need to develop good study habits. My two years at Masse went by very fast. After completing my technical training in June 1971, I was faced with another challenge of finding a job.

Because I attended trade school out of state, no one would hire me in my hometown. However, I did not give up or go back to working in the cotton mill. I joined the military and enlisted in the Air Force during the Vietnam War which despite the war turned out to be a great choice. Both of my uncles, Howard and Alfred Johnson, served in the Air Force and encouraged me to pursue my career with the Air Force. God was steering my decision. I met a gentleman named Jim Helman while in the Air Force. He was a 19-year veteran of the Air Force who was kicked out of the military because of his overweight condition. Jim was a very masculine man. He took me under his wings and taught me how to repair communication radios. Jim knew his stuff, and I was eager to learn since I was the only minority in the wideband communication field at my assigned squadron. Jim was the kind of gentleman that one could respect and appreciate. God orchestrated our pathways to meet and I've remained grateful that he sent someone to encourage me to succeed in life. Nevertheless, my time with Jim was only a year. As a young airman, he laid the foundation that later inspired me to return to school. Jim was my hero. He saw potential in me and inspired me and other young airman as well.

Encouraged to continue to learn my craft, I entered college after reenlisting in the Air Force. While stationed in Tinker Air Force Base, I began my college journey at Rose State College in Midwest City, Oklahoma in 1982. Having been out of school for quite some time, I didn't know if I could handle the rigors working full time and going to school part time. Rather than trying to take a full load, I began taking two or three courses per semester. I wanted to pursue an engineering degree. To my surprise, I was a model student thanks to Jim. In the military, I had to always be ready to be transferred. However, I was not discouraged, because I was focused and determined to reach my goal. After a one-year overseas tour to Istanbul, Turkey, I re-entered Rose State College only to remain there for another year before being transferring to Hampton, Virginia. After arriving at Langley Field, an Air Force base in Virginia, I began seeking engineering schools in the area. There was only one school in the area, Old Dominion University. Rather than applying to Old Dominion University and dealing with the high-volume traffic through the tunnel towards Norfolk, Virginia, I changed my major to mathematics with a minor in physics (pre-engineering). God must have been smiling because algebra, trigonometry and geometry were my worst subjects in school. God has a way of steering us in the right direction. I chose to attend Christopher Newport College to earn a Bachelor of Science Degree in mathematics with a minor in physics.

The course load was tremendous, and my weekends were filled with the demands of school. I was also very active in my church. Many of my fellow airmen enjoyed the nightclub scene. But, I chose to remain in my apartment writing software programs and working mathematical problems for class. I strived to grow and develop my mind; I enjoyed the time. The core of ignorance is stubbornness, and I did not want to waste my mind doing nothing.

I still remember the day I graduated from college, and it feels just like yesterday. Although my parents were not there, my wife and I celebrated my monumental accomplishment. To earn a degree in the very subject, mathematics, I struggled in high school with. With God's help all things are possible. When you take the information taught in class and consistently apply it, it breeds transformation in your character and self esteem.

Having obtained a Bachelor of Science Degree, I did not rest on my accomplishments. I sought to earn a Master of Science Degree in Management Information System from Bowie State. In the summer of 1997, I completed my degree requirements just before I retired from the U.S. Air Force. God orchestrated transition from the military to civilian life. In the summer of July 1997, my wife and I returned to Atlanta. It was time to seek employment outside of the military. I prepared my resumes with the help of the local transition representative from Fort McPherson. Within a month, I had more job offers than one could imagine. After consulting with my wife, we decided to remain in the Atlanta area. I accepted a position with Lockheed Martin Aeronautics Company.

While at Lockheed Martin, I learned that the individuals working at this defense contractor were highly motivated and incredibly smart. I made another decision that if I remain in the aeronautical business, I needed to retool myself. I began to pursue another Master's Degree in Technical Management Aeronautics. Most of my peers were pursuing advanced degrees to enhance their chances of getting promoted. Likewise, I joined the group entering into Embry Riddle Aeronautical University at Delta Airlines Training Facility. Those two and half years went by quickly, and I graduated in 2005. Since graduating from Embry Riddle, I have completed the Certified Reliability Engineering requirements from the American Society for Quality. I also earned a Certified Manager certificate from the Institute of Certified Managers at James Madison University. God works behind the scenes in helping us fulfill dreams in the midst of adversity.

Regardless of the adversities you may be experiencing in school or life, don't listen to the negative people that try to destroy your character. The very individuals who said that I was too dumb to be anything now look up to me as an inspiration. In closing, Dr. Edwin Louis Cole sums it up best, "The circumstances that surround a man's life are not important, his response to those circumstances is important. Because his response is the ultimate determining factor between success and failure."

I challenge you to remain teachable, and respect those teachers whose job is to present information to you for growth and development. Anything worth having in life doesn't always come easy, it takes a disciplined individual to pursue a dream. With God's help, pursue your dream!

INVICTUS
WILLIAM ERNEST HENLEY

Out of the night that covers me,
Black as the pit from pole to pole,
I thank whatever gods may be
For my unconquerable soul.

In the fell clutch of circumstance
I have not winced nor cried aloud.
Under the bludgeonings of chance
My head is bloody, but unbowed.

Beyond this place of wrath and tears
Looms but the Horror of the shade,
And yet the menace of the years
Finds and shall find me unafraid.

It matters not how strait the gate,
How charged with punishments the scroll,
I am the master of my fate,
I am the captain of my soul.

GET UP, PICK UP AND PRAY UP!

LAMONTE E. JONES

At the impressionable age of 17, I was summoned home to hear the most frightening news of my young life. I'm going to share that moment in time and the years that followed. What my mom did in the midst of a 23-year battle helped shape my life and prepare me for the giants I'd encounter along life's journey.

It was a typical, hot 90-degree June summer day in Chicago. School ended for the year and the most important thing on my mind was playing basketball and preparing for a senior year of high school that would earn me a sports scholarship to college. My junior year was solid, and expectations were high as college coaches began to express interest in me. Our team was favored to win the Blue-South Conference. Life was good for this 17-year-old, until all of a sudden the sky seemed to collapse on my world.

Mom called my older brother and I home from the park nearby. She explained to us that she was diagnosed with breast cancer. She was told by the doctors she was going to die. All of a sudden, dreams of going to college and playing basketball faded. Thoughts of life without a mother brought on a dark cloud of what my future would soon look like. To my amazement while the news of a seemingly near death situation entered my ears and mind for the first time, it was what mom said and did afterwards that gave me hope and a roadmap to a God-fearing, servant-leading and successful life.

Mom didn't spend time lying in bed feeling sorry for herself and asking God, "Why me at 37 years young?" She spent time encouraging the family and others while fighting through pain-filled days and bad news. She got knocked down several times hoping she was cured only to learn she needed a second, third and fourth surgery. She battled cancer for 23 years despite a six-month death prediction by doctors. Her faith told her, "God is the giver and taker of life," so she tarried on attempting to leave a legacy for her sons and would-be grandchildren to mimic. Each time she fell, she got up.

I watched mom struggle through many valley moments, yet she continued to climb. She persevered, prayed and patiently waited while standing on the promises of God. As a result, Mom was blessed to watch her sons graduate from college, marry, pursue their careers and birth her grandchildren. On a sunny Sunday afternoon, twenty-three years later from the time she received the cancer diagnosis, mom shared with me that she was tired and had fought a good fight. She died the next day. Clearly, God spoke to her and said, "Well done my good and faithful servant. You have endured, you have conquered, now is the time to rest and enjoy the victory."

Watching mom from age 17 to 40 taught me how to deal with life's crisis moments. Giants will come. God doesn't promise a world free from danger, but He does promise His help whenever we face danger. Psalm 91:1 states, "Those who live in the shelter of the Most High will find rest in the shadow of the Almighty."

When life knocks you down: Get up... stand, it's not the end! Pick up... your cross and walk! Pray up... to Christ, He answers!

> *All good men and women must take responsibility to create legacies that will take the next generation to a level we could only imagine.*
>
> — JIM ROHN

GOD HAS A PLAN LAID OUT FOR YOU

RUDOLPH JONES

Today we have a Black president. In the time when I was a boy, this was not even thought of. Young Black men did not have dreams of this magnitude. We were reared to be strong and take care of our families to the best of our ability. Providing for our family was our main concern rather than showing emotions or our feelings. So, I tried to do just that.

I married a girl from my hometown and joined the service. We were on our way. We moved north and started our family. We had four boys and two girls. My wife stayed home and took care of the children while I went to work. The years passed and our children grew up and moved on with their lives. They married and had their own children, got jobs, and bought houses. I retired and visited my children two or three times a year. Some of them lived in the south and some in the north. Everything was set, and things were going fine.

Well, God had a different path for me, a path that I never expected to go down. I found out that my youngest daughter had cancer. *How do you absorb that? When you raise your children and they finally make it out on their own, you think you have beaten the odds and everything is going to be fine. What does a father do for his child who has cancer? How do you fix or take care of that for them?* Well I thought she would be fine. *There are good doctors who will take care of her, and she will be fine.* This went on for over a year, doctors, doctors, and more doctors. However, I still thought she would be fine. It never entered my thoughts that she may die. She was young, just 44 years old, had a young daughter, she was strong, and surely she would get better.

It has been 10 years since my youngest daughter died from disease called cancer. I can see her face like it was yesterday. She was sitting right next to me. At times I still ask God, "Why, why my baby daughter?" See, my daughter was the glue in our family. We had holidays at her house. It was the

central meeting place when I came in town to visit. Not only was she gone, a way of life was gone too. Only God knows why this happened the way it did. It is not for me to question Him but to thank Him for the time we did have with her. We vowed to cherish the memories and good times and to know she had a special place in this world. That is what we hold on to. That is how we survived such a loss. God's ways are not our ways. We cannot out think God. Many times we do not understand the way He orchestrates our lives and the lives of the people we love.

Sometimes God will take you down a path that you had no idea you would go down. We must walk down that path with love, gratitude and praise.

> *The steps of a good man are ordered by the LORD, and He delights in his way.*
>
> PSALM 37:23

HARD WORK AND HONESTY BUILDS CHARACTER

GLADYS JORDAN

Mama and Daddy used to say:

1. Your word is your bond
2. Do a good job at whatever job you choose to do
3. Your name and reputation will travel much further than you will ever travel

I grew up in the 50s and 60s as the middle child of the late Mr. and Mrs. Otis Shaw Sr. My two sisters, two brothers and I grew up on a farm in Douglas, Georgia. My father was a sharecropper and my mother was a stay-at-home mom.

My parents were hard working and honest church-going people who taught the five of us that hard work and honesty builds character. We were also told that our name and reputation will travel much further than we will humanly travel. Also, they taught us that whatever job we chose to do, we should do it to the best of our abilities. If the job was digging a ditch, make sure that we dug the best ditch that could be dug.

My parents, who only had a grade school education, were determined that the five of us would continue our education after high school. They wanted us to follow in the footsteps of five of our cousins. Our cousins were four girls who had gone to college after high school to become school teachers, and our male cousin retired from the Army.

On Sunday evenings while visiting my grandparents, my grandfather farmed and cut pulpwood to survive. He would gather my sisters and brothers on the front porch and drill us about getting a good education and getting a trade so we would be able to support ourselves without help from anyone. Our parents were very proud of us because we all continued our education after high school. My two brothers, Otis Shaw Jr. and

Lacy Shaw, went off to Monroe Area Vocational Technical School in Albany, Georgia. They were trained in auto body and fender, and both are entrepreneurs today.

My older sister Willie M. Robinson graduated Albany State College after high school and retired from Clark Atlanta University Registrar's Office. She still works as a substitute teacher part time. My younger sister, Geneva S. Paulk, finished Dental Hygienists School in Atlanta and moved back to South Georgia. She was unable to pursue her career, because she could not find a job as a dental hygienist. There were only three dentists in town, and they were not hiring. In the late 60s, there were no Black dental hygienists in South Georgia.

I attended Monroe Area Vocational Technical School in Albany, the same school my brothers attended. I was given an opportunity to join the nursing program because the business program I applied for was full. I chose the nursing program because I did not want to go back home. I excelled in the program and was told by one of my instructors, Mrs. Estella Reynolds, that I should pursue my education to become a registered nurse. I graduated and passed my state board exam to become a licensed practical nurse (LPN).

I worked as an LPN for about five or six years. While working as an LPN at a local hospital, my supervisor, Sue Lewis Spivey, recognized my talents and told me I should go back to school to become a registered nurse (RN). There were no Black RNS working at the hospital during the late 60s. Sue challenged the hospital administrators for scholarship money for me to attend South Georgia College in Douglas. I graduated South Georgia College in June 1972 with an Associate's Degree in nursing. A few months later, I traveled to Atlanta to take the state board exam for registered nurses. I passed and became a certified registered nurse.

In 1989 after working as an RN for about 17 years, I decided I needed a salary increase. Going back to school to obtain a bachelor's degree in nursing (BSN) would position me for an increase in salary. My daughter, Krista Shinn, was in college at the time; therefore, I had a lot of spare time. At this time I was working in public health with the Fulton County Health Department. The director of nursing assisted me by allowing me to schedule my time so I could attend Clayton State College full time while working full time. I received my BSN Degree in June 1992. My student loans were mostly paid back through me working with Fulton County Health Department.

Working as a public health nurse was very satisfying and my salary increased, but I dreamed of something more. From the time of working as an LPN, I always enjoyed working with pregnant women, working in Labor and Delivery and working with newborn babies in the nursery. Fulton County Health Department needed obstetric-gynecological (OBGYN) nurse practitioners to serve women with women-related health concerns and prenatal care. My goal was to become an OBGYN nurse practitioner.

In the fall of 1992, I applied and was selected as a candidate for admission to the Emory University School of Medicine Regional Training Center for Family Planning and Women's Health. All expenses were paid.

This endeavor was like learning on steroids. This course was more intense than anything I ever encountered. I believe this is when I received most of my gray hair. We had an enormous amount of material that was very detailed and in depth to cover in limited time periods. After completing the preceptorship course and passing another State Board Exam, I became a certified OBGYN nurse practitioner on December 1995. During this period in my life I had two highly stressful events going on. My daughter experienced a fragile pregnancy and gave birth with complications to my first grandchild and I remarried for the second time.

My career in nursing became even more fulfilling while working as an OBGYN nurse practitioner until my retirement in 2001. Hard work was so ingrained in my genes that I spent another 13 years working with Kaiser Permanente and retired again in March 2015.

I give honor to God and my parents, the late Mr. and Mrs. Otis Shaw, Sr. for their love, belief in the Bible, hard work, honesty and words of wisdom. They brought five little children into this world and gave us what we needed to survive and succeed in our dreams and aspirations.

Psalm 27:1 states, "The Lord is my light and my salvation; whom shall I fear? The Lord is the strength of my life; of whom shall I be afraid?"

> *It is up to us to live up to the legacy that was left for us, and to leave a legacy that is worthy of our children and future generations.*
>
> CHRISTINE GREGOIRE

SURRENDER TO WIN

MARGOT JORDAN

I grew up believing that as adults, we were responsible to take care of ourselves and our families. I believed as an adult, this is what was required. I had a child out of wedlock at a young age. With the support of my family, I was able to attend college and landed a good job with the Eastman Kodak Company in Rochester, New York. I got married and proceeded to take care of my family as a wife and mother was supposed to, but my marriage didn't go well and I did not like living in Rochester. My family roots were in Georgia, so I wanted to go back. After five years, my marriage ended, and my daughter and I moved back to Georgia.

I reconnected with my childhood sweetheart and we eventually got married and blended our families. He had three children and I had one. I was able to transfer with Eastman Kodak in Georgia, so I was secure in providing for my family. In addition, my husband was a lieutenant for the City of Atlanta Fire Department. Things were going well. Often, we went to church and served God. As the years went on, we got away from going to church, and our marriage started getting into trouble. We separated after seven years.

Now, it was just my daughter and I. I worked a great deal because I needed to provide financially. However, I was unable to give her my time. As my daughter got older, she started hanging around groups of people who were headed for trouble. At an early age, she became pregnant and gave birth to my grandson. I badly wanted her to get on the right track, and I tried everything I could think of to help her do that. I paid her rent, bought her a car and even raised her son myself. None of that produced the results I hoped for. I was at the end of my rope and didn't know what to do.

During that time, my sister, who I was so close to, passed. The following year, my mother died and four years after that, my husband died. I really felt alone. I started seeking God for strength and guidance and heard, "We must surrender to win." I had no idea what that meant. For me, surrender meant losing and giving up. I was not a loser nor was I raised to give up. Through prayer and study, I learned that surrender meant to surrender to God and give him our cares and he would take care of us. It is not our job to fight our battles, but He will fight them for us. So I said, "God, I surrender. I give you my family to care for. I will serve and praise You; I will 'walk by faith, not by sight." I involved myself in a closer relationship with God. I trusted His Word and tithed. I learned that God is faithful and He loves and cares for us.

I focused on going back to school, and I graduated cum laude with my master's degree in Accounting. I raised my grandson to love and trust God. I told him that God will take care of his mother. My daughter has changed her whole life around. We own a business together, and she is there for me and her son. God has shown me that if I surrender and trust him, He will take my cares and will work all things together for good. Surrender to win and God will take care of you!

> *Father, if it is Your will, take this cup away from me; nevertheless not my will, but Yours, be done.*
>
> LUKE 22:42

A GIFT OF LIFE AND A SECOND CHANCE

ALICE MARSHALL

It started one cool fall night. I was out playing softball and preparing to bat next. The pitcher pitched the ball; I hit it and took off running full speed to first base. Once I reached the base, I felt like I was having a heart attack. I decided to put myself out of the game and take a rest in the dug-out. After the game was over, I went home and got some rest. The next morning, I was up straightening the bathroom when my chest began hurting again. I decided I should go to the hospital. Upon my arrival, the hospital staff immediately took me to the back for tests and observations. One test came back stating I had walking pneumonia. They decided to keep me longer and ran more tests, a shadow kept showing up in the tests. The doctors referred me to a lung doctor. Once I met the lung doctor, his team took a biopsy which revealed that I had a lung disorder called Sarcoidosis. This is a disorder that causes scar tissue on the lungs. I knew something was wrong and it had to be fixed!

As I lived with this disorder for years without ever going into remission, I continued to keep God first in this ordeal. Eventually, my condition worsened, and I knew the only thing that could possibly save me was God and a lung transplant. During my appointment with my lung doctor, he sat down to give me the news of my condition. He told me I would need a transplant, and if I didn't get one, I would only have about two years to live. I was shocked and sad about this news. Then, I remembered the scripture, Psalm 4:1, "Hear me when I call, O God of my righteousness: thou hast enlarged me when I was in distress; have mercy upon me, and hear my prayer." So when I left the doctor's office, I threw my hands up and told God this battle is too big for me to handle, I give it all to you.

Later that week I returned to Emory Hospital for an appointment. I found out I was a great candidate for a transplant. That was great news, but I ran into an issue because I couldn't receive the transplant at Emory due to Emory being an experiment hospital. I was given three other choices, Durham, North Carolina, Birmingham, Alabama, or Washington D.C. I chose Birmingham since it was the closer to my home.

The real journey began next; I endured a week of testing from my head to my feet. The test ensured I was in a sound mind before the transplant. I was issued a pager which was used to inform me when a donor match was found. I had two false alarms, but when the final page came through, my life changed forever. My husband and I flew down I-20 making it to the hospital in enough time to find out I was definitely a match for this lung. The team of doctors prepped me, and I immediately went into surgery. On February 27, 2000, I received my "gift of life and a second chance!" I knew on the day I gave it to the Lord, He would answer my prayer. Psalm 23:1 states, "The Lord is my Shepard I shall not want."

Despite the seven to nine year life-span expectancy for a transplant patient, I've exceeded that. I am on year 15. Praise God! I've had my battles, but they have always belonged to the Lord. I've had pneumonia many, many times yet I still stand all because of God's grace and mercy.

I thank God every day for His grace and mercy and for blessing me with a second chance of life for 15 years. If you believe it, you shall receive it!

> *I shall not die, but live, and declare the works of the Lord.*
>
> PSALM 118:17

MY LIVING SPEAKS

FANNIE MOORE MAY

I was born in Crenshaw County in Luverne, Alabama. I attended Helicon High School and completed 12th grade as valedictorian. I was chosen as homecoming queen in Dothan, Alabama, the day President John F. Kennedy was assassinated. I attended Massey Business College and married my first boyfriend and high school sweetheart. We had five children, four girls and one son, which included twin girls. All of our girls' names start with a V: Valerie, Verna, Veronica (the twins) and Valencia. My son was named after his father, Nelson Fitzgerald. I had five beautiful girls and one handsome son.

All the girls were Miss Football at Luverne High School. Valerie ran for Miss Luverne High. She won, but because she was Black, it was not given to her. One of her best friends who was White told her that she had the most votes. My husband was Deacon at our home church, Helicon Missionary Baptist. I served as secretary before and after we built the new church.

Our house burned, and we lost everything. Thanks to God we didn't die in the fire. We only had our pajamas on, and we were all asleep when the fire started. We found ourselves homeless with five children. It was like a death. Before the house burned we owned a grocery store, a used car lot and a laundromat. After our home burned, my husband and I divorced. I moved to Georgia May 21, 1984. I got a job at Bank of America and stayed there 16 years. I started working there when it was known as CES Bank. In 1999, the Trust Department was bought out by New York Trust. I was one of the people they asked to move to New York, but I didn't go.

After that, I worked for Wellstar Cobb Hospital and have been there for over 15 years. Working there is my ministry. Patients and employees use to give me angels. I put them all in my office and I was asked to take them down because they were in a place where people could see them. I put my *Daily Word* out, so patients and employees can read them daily. My passion is people. I love people. I love to cook sweet potato pies, corn bread, collard greens, kale, turnip and mustard greens together. I make a great banana pudding. I get a joy out of giving. My youngest daughter calls me Mother Teresa and my previous minister, Minister Beckford, called me Esther.

My life story is not about me. Everything I do is for kingdom living. My prayer is, "May the life I live speak for me. May my living not be in vain." I just want to help someone as I travel along my way.

> *Everybody can be great... because anybody can serve.*
> *You don't have to have a college degree to serve.*
> *You don't have to make your subject and verb agree to serve.*
> *You only need a heart full of grace.*
> *A soul generated by love.*
>
> Dr. Martin Luther King, Jr.

USE ME LORD

MARGARET WILSON MCCORMICK

At this writing, I am 92 years young. I remember growing up; I was the only one on the "team of helping others." I would often get into trouble with my mother for giving my lunch away to students and quite honestly some teachers as well. Listen, my mama could cook and they all knew it. As a result, I learned that this posture of servanthood would soon lead me to my career passion, to teach, share and help others see that there was more inside of them to discover. It became my passion to, "rescue" them from themselves and unleash a world of possibilities!

I've traveled to 28 countries, worked with and initiated several mission-driven projects from collecting hundreds of thousands of empty medicine bottles for Haiti to leading a charge that has resulted in collecting over one million shoes for African nations and other third-world countries. As a retired principal, I'm an educator for life, always learning and always willing to share with others who may need to be "rescued" from their small thinking. At a time in history, with great challenge, I was fortunate enough to attend Columbia University, the Atlanta University Center and Fort Valley State University to prepare for my future. I have seen almost a century of living. For the past 28 years, I've worked as a college-campus minister at my undergraduate alma mater, Fort Valley State University. This opportunity came after retiring from 40 years of education. It kept me engaged with college students. Their horizons were broadened when I took them to Germany and many other countries to serve as global ambassadors, once again expanding their world view and encouraging growth and life's possibilities. The following passage is truly my life's mission.

1 Corinthians 13 New International Version

If I speak in the tongues of men or of angels, but do not have love, I am only a resounding gong or a clanging cymbal. ² If I have the gift of prophecy and can fathom all mysteries and all knowledge, and if I have a faith that can move mountains, but do not have love, I am nothing. ³ If I give all I possess to the poor and give over my body to hardship that I may boast, but do not have love, I gain nothing.

⁴ Love is patient, love is kind. It does not envy, it does not boast, it is not proud. ⁵ It does not dishonor others, it is not self-seeking, it is not easily angered, it keeps no record of wrongs. ⁶ Love does not delight in evil but rejoices with the truth. ⁷ It always protects, always trusts, always hopes, always perseveres.

⁸ Love never fails. But where there are prophecies, they will cease; where there are tongues, they will be stilled; where there is knowledge, it will pass away. ⁹ For we know in part and we prophesy in part, ¹⁰ but when completeness comes, what is in part disappears. ¹¹ When I was a child, I talked like a child, I thought like a child, I reasoned like a child. When I became a man, I put the ways of childhood behind me. ¹² For now we see only a reflection as in a mirror; then we shall see face to face. Now I know in part; then I shall know fully, even as I am fully known.

¹³ And now these three remain: faith, hope and love. But the greatest of these is love.

After reminiscing on this anecdote and listing to a few of the many things that are a great part of my life and who I am today, I truly "Thank God For My Journey" now and I want him to continue to "Use Me" for His service!

Use Me, O Lord

For Thee, Lord a cross I'll bear, and I'll go anytime, anywhere.
I'll not falter from the weight of woe, if you lead me Lord, I'll go.

Use me, Lord, use me for Thy glory, Use me Lord, help me tell love's story
make my will obey, use me Lord, I'll go all the way, use me Lord I pray.

*For we are
His workmanship,
created in Christ Jesus
for good works,
which God prepared beforehand
that we should walk in them.*

EPHESIANS 2:10

ASK GOD FOR THE ANSWER

JOANN MCNEAR

What a friend we have in Jesus, all our sins and grief to bear. What a privilege it is to carry everything to God in prayer.

Around 40 years ago, I experienced a very unsettling situation concerning the mysterious movements of my car. I would like to share how the spirit of the all-knowing God solved the mystery.

I was newly divorced living with my two children in Chicago in a two-family brick building where we lived for about five years. The landlord lived on the bottom level along with her family, including a teenage son whom I had a good relationship with.

On occasion my girlfriend and I would stop on Friday's after work for a glass of wine or two. One Saturday morning as I left to go to work, I noticed my car was not where I parked it. I was always able to get a parking spot very close to the apartment, but this morning it was down the street. After arriving to work still very perplexed concerning my car, I mentioned it to the police officer, who was a friend of mine, and he thought it was hilarious. He asked if my friend, Gwen, and I stopped after work and had more than two glasses of wine. I said, "I know where I parked my car."

The following Saturday morning my car was parked in a different location than where I parked it, again. That's when I knew I had to go to God in prayer about this situation.

Meanwhile, I had no clue or explanation concerning this mystery, however I knew who did, and asked Him to show me who was moving my car. I thanked him, because He immediately responded to my need. In a dream, He showed me my landlord's teenage son and his friend getting out of my car. Sometime ago I allowed him to go and wash my car, and he must have had a key made without my consent.

Friday night my landlord, her son and I were saying our goodnights. As I was leaving, I looked out of this big picture window on the landing. Just as the Lord showed me, my landlord's teenager and his friend was parking my car in the exact place I parked.

I learned, no matter what seems too difficult for me, nothing is too difficult for God. We have to trust in Him with our heart and lean not on our own understanding. And in all our ways acknowledge Him, and He will direct our paths.

Ask, and it will be given to you; seek, and you will find; knock, and it will be opened to you.

MATTHEW 7:7

MY JESUS, MY JOURNEY

BLANCHE MILLS

What an awesome God we serve. I was born in the Deep South in a very small, country town in the good state of North Carolina some 74 years ago. I am the third oldest of six children. At an early age somewhere between the ages of six and seven, I began to pay attention to my parents and grown-ups as they disciplined me. They were not always correct and fair.

I really loved going to Sunday school and church. However, my siblings didn't seem as interested. They would get upset with me because of my willingness to go, and they were forced to go also. There was something that amazed me about the teachings of God and Jesus in Sunday school and especially learning that there was someone over my mom and dad and all adults.

I knew it had to be God, Himself. Mom and dad had nothing to do with God's creations: night and day, the blue skies, white clouds, wind, rain and seasons changing from winter to summer. This really blew my mind. I began to study all the information I could find about this God that no one could see or hear. My church family at AME Zion thought I had a special calling. I didn't understand what they were speaking about. All I knew was that I loved learning. I began teaching Sunday school at age 13. How awesome was that?

At age 15, I entered high school but realized that the majority of students were not interested in God, so I continued serving Him privately while participating in high school activities which were good and enjoyable. Then the unexpected happen. My oldest brother died of a massive heart attack at age 19 after football practice at Syracuse University. What a blow and a shock to the whole town. At his funeral, there were just as many Whites as Blacks and as many people on the outside as on the inside of the small, country church.

He was one of the most loved and perfect human beings that I've ever known. He was almost like a mother and father to me. At 15 years old, almost 16, I didn't really think about losing a family member. This was very painful. Anger began to grow more and more in me to the point where I stopped going to church and stopped praying. I became so angry at God. Why did He take someone that was kind, loving and perfect and leave behind all the mean,

liquor-drinking, wife beaters and nasty-talking men to live? Five or six months later, I realized I didn't like God anymore. One Sunday after church, my pastor came to my house and asked me to go for a walk with him. His voice seemed different. It was kind, quiet and soft spoken. He said to me, "Do you know that Jesus loves you? Do you know that Jesus loved your brother? Do you know that Jesus feels your pain, Apple (my nickname)?" He said, "God told me to tell you that your brother is fine, and he is happy where he is."

As we walked, my pastor stated that God was in control of everything, and I may not understand it now, but would understand later in life. He explained that God can handle any anger I had towards Him, and God was not upset with me. He told me not to let my anger continue. I asked my pastor, "Why did God take my brother?" And he replied, "God does not make mistakes, and neither you or your family are being punished, but that was part of God's will. We may never know why, but God loves us very much." It took some time but I slowly began to reach out to God. I told God I forgave Him, "…because I know You don't make mistakes." I asked Him to forgive me. Don't we serve a mighty God?

Upon completing high school, I entered Bennett College, a girls-only school, in Greensboro, North Carolina. After completing two years, I transferred to Winston-Salem State University and promptly graduated. Prior to leaving Bennett College, I was fortunate to meet Thurgood Marshall and Martin Luther King Jr. After graduating from Winston-Salem, my parents granted me a two-week vacation to New York, the, "Big Apple." I moved to New York and stayed for 21 years and worked at PS 35, a public school, and for the New York Department of Human Resources as a certified children's counselor. That was the most gratifying job I've ever had. I got married in New York, and we were blessed with one daughter, Latarsha. In 1985, I moved to Atlanta where I was employed with the State of Georgia and Fulton County Superior Court for 16 years. I am retired and enjoying every minute of it. Latarsha is married and has two sons, the oldest, Amir, is a senior at Stillman College in Alabama where he has maintained the honor roll since entering college. He plans to continue his education in pharmaceutical studies. The youngest, Jalal, is 11 years old in the 6th grade. He is very active in his academics and basketball. God has continuously blessed me and my family throughout the years. We are walking in His blessings as the journey continues. I now thank God for everything and encourage you to do the same.

> *For My thoughts are not your thoughts, nor are your ways My ways, says the LORD.*
>
> ISAIAH 55:8

THINGS CHANGE

ANITA RAMSEY MINNIEFIELD
COLONEL, U.S. ARMY RETIREE

I had no intention of joining the Army when I went off to the University of Georgia in August 1975. In fact, I planned to become a school teacher just like my mother. Things change. My eyes were opened when I was left alone with my mama's fourth grade class. It was during my spring break. So, I switched my major to journalism. At the end of my sophomore year, for some reason, I joined Army ROTC. The reason was money. If I went to summer school between sophomore and junior year, took ROTC classes, at the start of my junior year, I would receive an ROTC stipend – money! I attended summer school and took the necessary classes. At the beginning of my junior year, I signed the ROTC contract. The contract was binding, but I wanted the money. I rationalized and decided to simply join the U.S. Army Reserve. Again, I wanted the money. I became an Army ROTC cadet. I was so not interested in the military, the Army or the drills. What had I gotten myself into? But, I got the money-each and every month. I attended the classes and performed the drills. I managed to evade the bivouacs and was a mediocre cadet. But I got the money.

Between my junior and senior year, cadets attended an ROTC summer camp for six weeks at hot and sandy Fort Bragg, North Carolina. Those were the worst six weeks of my entire life and still are. I should have paid attention to more than the money. After barely passing camp and surviving those six weeks, I made a decision immediately. I requested active duty rather than the Reserve, because I figured nothing else in the Army could be as bad as summer camp and nothing was.

I was commissioned a second lieutenant in May 1979. I entered active duty with a three-year commitment. I truly planned to only do three years and get out. Things change. My first duty station was the Military District of Washington with duty at Ft. Myer in Arlington, Virginia. During those three years, I grew up a lot. I had more responsibilities as a 21-year-old lieutenant than I ever had in life. I discovered that the Army was okay, and maybe I'd do a couple more years. When I ran into any of my former ROTC buddies, they would ask with disbelief, "You still in the Army?" Things change.

Ft. Myer was followed by a year in Korea, school in Indianapolis, and then to Ft. Stewart, Georgia. In 1985 I met and married my husband Robert Minniefield. We had a whirl-wind romance. We started dating in August and married in November. We went from Ft. Stewart to Korea, school in Kansas with a new baby girl, and then to Washington, DC. I became pregnant with another baby girl, then to Korea again. Somewhere along the way, I became a military officer. I was promoted to colonel in 2002 and served a total of 26 years of active duty. I retired in 2005. And to think, it all started because I wanted that ROTC money, $100 a month. Things really do change.

> *To improve is to change;*
> *to be perfect is to change often.*
>
> WINSTON CHURCHILL

POWER IN LOVE

EVANGELIST CURTIS AND PROPHETESS BOBBIE MINTER

We have been married 13 years, and we met online. On our first phone call our spirits were united, and there was nothing we could do about it. It was a spiritual connection from the start. Our verse is Psalms 34:8, "O taste and see the Lord is good…" I, Curtis tasted Bobbie's spirit through her voice, and I knew in my heart I found truly what I needed for the rest of my life. She did too, even though we didn't say it at first. We dated and courted for four months and decided to never exit our honeymoon phase.

In September 1999 we founded Real Life International Mission Inc. (RLIM), a Georgia-based 501(c)3 non-profit, evangelistic organization. We have taken over 30 mission trips in the past 20 years witnessing over 40,000 people come to Christ. We have an overwhelming passion to reach the lost and empower people from all walks of life.

A few years ago God gave us a witty invention. We call it, "Power-In-Names" (P.I.N.). Basically, He gave us the ability to enrich the lives of people by showing them the power in their God-given names. What's in the depths of your God-given name? Could you imagine a world without names? What would we call places, things or objects? What would we call each other? How would we communicate? Names carry powerful meanings. The question is, are we living out our namesake? Every person needs to know their purpose and identity in the Body of Christ. Your name is a powerful tool as you develop and grow in Christ. The two major gifts you will experience after we speak over your name are prophecy and word of knowledge. You will have a better understanding with confirmation toward your destiny in life.

Here's an example of how God allowed us to perceive the meaning of Seasoned Saints.

You may ask, what is a Seasoned Saint? A Seasoned Saint is not about age. It is a class of people who truly know their current season. Seasoned Saints are individuals who are sinners but have become a saint that occasionally sins. We, as Christians, should call each other Saint Mary, Saint Joe or whatever your name is, but instead we

call each other Brother, Sister, etc. People are not perfect, but they 'se-a-son' (see-a-son). It's in the word, 'season'. When you see-a-son, when you see Jesus, you know that you are in your season. Let's take it a little further. After you see Jesus ('seas' Him), you take a hold of Him and then you can go into the depths with Him, the 'sea', the deep things of God. The 'a-s' in the middle of 'season,' stands for, "'as' you speak it," and "'as' you declare it."

Seasoned Saints truly know Him and have been preserved to taste and see that the Lord is good. They have been seasoned to the taste of Christly things as they share their stories. Let's look at the word 'saint.' If we are not really lined up with the Word of God and true salvation, remove the, 's' from saints, you have, 'aints.' Many Christians are 'aints' because they do not fully believe and trust the Word of God.

As you grow in Christ – it is our prayer that you will trust in Him and let His Word season you for this season in your life.

> *You are the salt of the earth; but if the salt loses its flavor, how shall it be seasoned?*
> *It is then good for nothing but to be thrown out and trampled underfoot by men.*
>
> MATTHEW 5:13

PERCEPTION OF MARRIAGE

LEON AND ANGELIA NOBLE

O k, let's talk! We have something to say. No, not just anything, something important! We want to help you girl! Man, we got you! No worries – we got you!

We are Leon and Angelia Noble. We married on December 3, 1983, on a cold and rainy day in Atlanta, Georgia. We have a handsome son named Jonathan who is a junior at Kennesaw State University. Leon is an Information Technologist and Angelia is the financial bookkeeper for the district of DeKalb County Schools. Yes, we are "regular people," but, we are experts in the area of what not to do in a marriage or relationship. We're going to share with you a little bit about the beginning, middle and almost ending of our marriage. We're going to share the secret stuff.

What makes a good marriage? The same thing that makes a bad marriage: perception. Perception is a way of regarding, understanding, or interpreting something; a mental impression.

In the beginning, our first few months or even years together were very good. Because we got along so well, we decided to get married. We were both in the Navy which is a job with great benefits, without a care in the world. At one point along the way, we were unable to cope with each other's personalities or habits. The things about me, Angelia, that were once cute to Leon were no longer cute. And at the time – I had to ask myself what happened to the Leon who always wanted to do everything I wanted to do? A change in perception happened. The honeymoon was over and our masks were removed.

It is human nature to be self-oriented and self-absorbed. We believe that our selfishness got in the way of us really respecting each other. We began projecting our thoughts, feelings and experiences on each other. We did not think about each other's feelings. Our actions as result of negative and wrong thinking gave birth to moments of disappointment.

I believed that Leon should always cheer me up and be there when I needed him to be. But surprisingly enough, it was not the shift of focus from "me" to "us" that gave us a hard time. The real difficulty was judging each other based on perception versus based on facts. I mean, when I pictured marriage, I didn't picture me picking up Leon's clothes all the time. During that time, Leon was often gone due to the Navy. Returning home from another country was a big deal. Coming home from an eight-to-five job just doesn't have the same level of excitement.

Back in the day, I was a knockout. I used to wait at the pier looking sexy for my man when he returned after being out to sea for sixty days at a time. But as the years passed, things changed and I failed to look the way I did prior to marriage. It took a minute to learn that you have to do the same thing you did to get him to keep him.

As a man, I was under the impression that we should just fall into our roles as husband and wife. I quickly learned that there is no mold to fall into. You must get to know your spouse and accept them for who they are. I learned that being married was not a one-sided ordeal. It has to be a team effort. My perception in the beginning was that once I made my request to my wife known – she would carry them out and everything would be all-right. Later on in our marriage, I learned that things must be discussed and an agreement has to be met regarding the direction of the relationship. This, "eureka moment" came after many arguments and a brief separation.

Living apart for nine months was the worse and best thing that happened to us. No, separation is ever God's perfect will, but it was the best time with God that I ever had. God showed me with clarity that I was lost. Yes, you heard me right. My perception of who I was and what I deserved as a woman was way off. I would cry out to God in the middle of the night. I asked Him to restore me.

Through it all, I remembered that He loved and He cared for me. And I firmly believed that He would never put more on me than I could bear. Finally I let go and let God be God in my life. I began reading His Word and searching out scriptures relating to self-perception.

My mind was made up, and I was feeling pretty good about my next move. I was all cried out and divorce was imminent despite the fact that our son desperately needed us. Then, one day while standing in the court house, my lawyer says to me, "I've been doing this for 15 years and I don't believe your husband wants a divorce." God used a Christian divorce lawyer to bring me to a turning point that would save my marriage. It became evident that in order to establish a better life with my wife I had to let go of unhealthy beliefs and rely on what I've learned. On December 3, 2015, we will happily celebrate 33 years of marriage!

*Love consists of not looking each other in the eye,
but of looking outwardly in the same direction.*

ANTOINE DESAINT

HOW TO HAVE A HAPPY MARRIAGE

ROBERT AND JOYCE NORWOOD

I met my wife of 48 years through a friend who asked if I could pick his girlfriend up from the Atlanta City Auditorium. She was fulfilling a high school assignment of listening to an aspiring presidential candidate, Senator Hubert Humphrey.

My friend's girlfriend and her best friend were walking from the auditorium down a street known for its ill-reputed vices. But, to this very day, my wife claims the street we met on was another street. However, we met and my thoughts turned into action immediately, not about marriage, but what could be gained from this introduction?

I was an 18-year-old freshman at Morehouse College. She was a 16-year-old junior at David T. Howard High School. We began a relationship without marriage in mind. After dating for about a year, we decided to marry due to noticeable circumstances.

At the time, I was a member of Ebenezer Baptist and we asked Rev. Martin Luther King, Sr. to marry us, and he refused. He said we were too young and did not know what we were doing. One of the assistant pastors married us at his home with only our mothers, my fiancée's best friend and my best friend present. We enjoyed cookies and punch for the reception. The honeymoon weekend was at the Holiday Inn in Downtown Atlanta.

My wife joined Ebenezer Baptist with me. She thought early on to put God first, and believed that a family that prays together and worships together stays together. We became faithful servants in the church together. In our early years of marriage, my wife was more mature, and in some instances, smarter than me (even though I was older). It took many years to catch up in smartness and maturity.

Ten years later, Rev. Martin Luther King, Sr. surprisingly asked us to stand up after a church service. He apologized for not marrying us. He said, "Seeing you all still together with a family and working together as a team is a blessing." This is a cherished and unforgettable moment for us. You see, we did know what we were doing.

After 34 years at Ebenezer Baptist, God led us to Word of Faith Cathedral Worship Center. We wondered what took us so long. Our early years of marriage were no different than other marriages. Financial problems and vigorous exchanges of descending ideas, and as Bishop Dale C. Bronner would say, "…not speaking or touching while sleeping in the same bed." After three or four days without contact, we began to wonder how to make up without saying, "I am sorry."

After years of going around the same mountain, we decided we didn't want to be right all the time. We just wanted to be happy. We learned to say, "I am sorry," even though the other person may have been at fault. We relearned how to become friends. We learned to respect each other. We learned that marriage is a process with progress. We learned how to set short-term goals with long-term plans and how to temper our expectations with thought and prayer. We learned how to change the, "me" to "we." We learned that marriage is a covenant not a contract.

That covenant was, "To have and to hold from this day forward, for better or for worse, for richer, for poorer, in sickness and in health, to love and to cherish from this day forward until death do us part."

Mark 10:8-9 states, "And the two will become one flesh. So they are no longer two, but one flesh. Therefore, what God has joined together let no one separate."

We thank God for two wonderful children and four delightful grandchildren. These are the rules we live by in our home.

1. A family that prays together stays together.
2. God's favor is better than silver and gold.
3. He gives you joy unspeakable joy.
4. You may not see a way because he is the way.
5. Not my will but your will be done.
6. Whatever you are, try to be a good one.
7. If you can't say something good about someone, don't say anything at all.
8. We learned how to continue waiting and hoping, waiting and praying and waiting and expecting, because Jesus Christ is now the Alpha & Omega in our lives.

Marriage may be the closest thing to Heaven or Hell any of us will know on earth.

EDWIN LOUIS COLE

SERVING HIM WITH HYMNS AND DEEDS

RUTH SCHOFIELD PARKER

I began my singing career at an early age in the Apostolic Church of Christ of Bishop William Parker. My father was the pastor. My mother, Lina Parker, encouraged me to sing. A God-sent woman prophesied to my mother that I would be a chosen vessel to praise God in the ministry of music. Because of my mother's prayers, I stayed close to the Almighty God and totally committed my life to praising Him.

I received national attention in the gospel world as the featured soloist with the famed Clinton Utterbach Concert Ensemble. We sang soul-stirring selections such as, "Hold Back the Night" and "Get in Touch With Heaven." I have recorded with the Greater Bible Way Temple of Brooklyn, New York, as lead singer on Michael Rogers composition, "Stay With God." I consider it a blessing and privilege to record my first album with Reverend Doctor James Cleveland, the undisputed King of Gospel.

God also used me to create a vibrant and effective children's ministry. The ministry is crucial to the well-being and longevity of West Angeles Church of God in Christ in Los Angeles, California. The Children's Department allowed us to reach our kids and the unchurched by creating a safe and appealing Christian environment. The department consisted of the Nursery, Preschool, Girl and Boy Scouts, the Angelic Choir, Children's Church, Children's Bible Study, Children's Nutrition and Aerobics, Children's Drama and Vacation Bible School. My staff and dedicated volunteers have implemented CPR classes for volunteer workers, a foster and adoptive parent support group, Teens Church, Teens Members Class, Children's Tuesday Evening Bible Study, Preschool Cap and Gown Graduation and a Nursery and Preschool Teachers Thank You Celebration. According to a crowning report, 139 children accepted Christ as their savior. Some save the whales, and that's a good thing, but we specialize in saving our children.

Through my unwavering love, commitment and leadership, I've led thousands of young and old to the transforming and healing power found in Jesus Christ. Ministries for youth and children were established and currently flourish with over 15 separate auxiliaries that specifically cater to the spiritual and psychological maturation and development of children. In my transition from Los Angeles to Atlanta, I became a member of Word of Faith (WOF), serving as a hostess. My desire is that all people that enter WOF see my smiling face and experience a warm heart. Upon their leaving, I strive to leave an impression that cannot be erased.

The legacy I desire to leave behind is the strong belief that our present generation will not fall through the cracks, be ignored or forgotten. This legacy will carry to the next generation. I leave this legacy to my one and only son, Derrick Schofield, so that he will continue in his anointing and carry on the family music legacy.

> *But Jesus said, let the little children come to Me, and do not forbid them; for of such is the kingdom of heaven.*
>
> MATTHEW 19:14

JUST KEEP HAVING BIRTHDAYS

MARY PEEKS

"Just keep having birthdays," my daddy used to say.

He was the father of 15 children. Sometimes, when questions were asked or comments were made about why he did something we didn't understand, he would say, "Just keep having birthdays." Back home we sang the song, "We'll Understand it Better By and By." We thought it meant, "…when we die." No. When you are young, old peoples' words and actions do not make any sense.

Now, I find myself smiling, talking aloud, crying and shouting. See, God has been good to me.

At age three I was burned with hot grease. I never went to the doctor and never had a scar. From age three to 10, I was sexually molested. At age 10, I moved to Georgia. I was in the 1st grade. I graduated at 19 and married someone who mentally and physically abused me; I had low self-esteem. In the 60s, married with four children, my husband divorced me for his bisexual lifestyle.

During my first of five admissions to a mental hospital, I thought, "It's not over yet. Just keep having birthdays."

On January 1, 1968, as I returned home from visiting my sister at the hospital, I was hit by a drunk driver. I went through the windshield, and my face was lacerated, broken bones and I was pronounced dead on arrival. God said, "No, there will be more birthdays."

Five years later, I met and married Mr. Peek and had two more children. When I became pregnant with the second baby, the doctor told my husband that he may lose the baby and me. I underwent an emergency surgery. During the next 12 months, blood clots formed in my legs. I also developed venous ulcers in both legs. I developed cancer in my veins and the doctor said I was about to lose my left leg.

Between high school and marriage, I attended Beauty College and mastered Cosmetology. I

Mary T. Peek

owned my own shop. Trying to be nice, I let some undesirables into my shop, and I knew it would get out of control.

I was newly established at the church in East Point (Word of Faith). One Sunday, the message was, "Just say no." During the altar call, I was the first one up. God helped me to, "Just say no." I was in a rush to get to church and didn't dress my wounds or find a clean skirt. There were beauty shop stains on my skirt. After prayer, Pastor Dale Bronner called me and another lady to step out of the crowd. I was furious. He kept on until I obediently stepped out. I was trying to hide the sores on one leg while using my other hand to conceal the stains on my skirt.

And of course, he told us to raise our hands high. He touched my head and prayed for my health. I wanted to scream, "Leave my legs alone!" I wanted to, "Just say no." Dismayed and embarrassed, I went home and kept my legs dressed. A few days later, I gathered some supplies and sat down to remove the bandages. I screamed! Everybody look, look. There were no sores on either leg. I used to believe what God would do, now I know. Just keep having birthdays. Thirty-five years later my legs are still healed. I am here for a season and for a reason until there are no more birthdays

> *So I will restore to you the years that the swarming locust has eaten,*
> *The crawling locust,*
> *The consuming locust,*
> *And the chewing locust,*
> *My great army*
> *which I sent among you.*
>
> JOEL 2:25

GREATNESS ERUPTS

PRESTON PENN

I was born December 26, 1960, to Captain Percy and Jeanne Penn. I was born in Wareham, Massachusetts. My family was stationed at Otis Air Force Base. I was the fifth child born into a loving and nurturing family. In order to understand what lies ahead of me, I have to look at my family's past.

My father was a son of sharecroppers, David and Mabel Penn, who lived in Daphne, Alabama (Baldwin County). My father left the farm in 1948 and entered Tuskegee Institute. He became a member of the Tuskegee Airmen and graduated in 1952. He met my mother who also attended Tuskegee as a nursing student. Her parents were James A. and Beulah C. Johnson of Tuskegee Institute. Her parents were considered a part of the "Black Elite" of their day and both very active in the politics of Alabama and the South. My grandfather was a banker, and my grandmother an educator. Because of my lineage, I desired to be "of service" not only within my community but also in the surrounding politics.

During my childhood, we moved to Ohio where my father was a student at the Air Force Institute of Technology in 1963. Then, in 1964 we moved to Nellis Air Force Base in Las Vegas where my brother Percy was born. We moved several more times to the Philippines, back to Tuskegee while my dad was stationed in Vietnam and eventually to Topeka, Kansas. The move to Topeka transformed my life. After my dad retired in 1972, I was old enough to realize my world was beginning to unravel. I used to hear my parents fighting and arguing. Even though my parents were religious and attended church, (my father was a Baptist and my mother was Catholic as were we) the damages from the war and effects of alcoholism was too much to bear. War has an evil and damaging effect on one's soul. I saw the changes within my dad when we met him at Maxwell Air Force Base upon his return from Vietnam in 1969. He even walked differently. My mom and dad divorced shortly after his discharge from the military in 1972, and life for me forever changed. After the divorce I used to listen to Wayne Newton's, "Daddy Don't You Walk So Fast," over and over again, crying because I needed my father in my life. I was becoming a teenager, and I needed wisdom and advice from him. My mother was unable to understand what was going on in the mind of a preteen or teenager no matter how hard she tried. We always had a close-knit family (even with our extended family), but the perils of war do not stop on the battlefield. Just like blood oozes from a dying man, it also destroys the fabric of the family. War changes a man from within.

I attended Most Pure Heart of Mary from fourth until eighth grade. Besides my siblings, the only other Blacks who attended were the Casons. They lived in an orphanage next to the school. During these years I was called "the N word" by a white classmate. First, I was called "the N word" in fourth grade. I gave the boy a chance to apologize. He didn't so punishment had to come swiftly! I beat him, and this is when I learned that justice is not fair. I was suspended and he was not. This continued once a year all the way until ninth grade at Hayden High. After ninth grade my mom sent me across town to Highland Park. Topeka High was still reeling from Brown v. Topeka Board of Education, so the schools still suffered a lot of racial tension. It was quite a different experience at Highland Park. I hadn't been in a predominantly Black school since attending St. Joseph's Catholic in Tuskegee Institute. Here, I learned a different lesson. I graduated in 1979 and enrolled in North Carolina Central University. It was not my plans to attend college right away as I was not mentally prepared. Even though my siblings attended college (Duke University and University of Kansas), I had scars from my teenage years that needed to be healed. See, I was just becoming a teenager when my dad left. Once he departed we had very little contact until I became an adult. As a child, I was wrongly influenced in life. I started smoking marijuana and having sex at the age of 13. A recipe of disaster consists of no guidance from a father and a mom who was forced to go back to work to support her six children. I eventually left college in 1983 and joined the Army. I should have chosen that path straight out of high school. I needed the discipline I sorely lacked in life.

My mother, who was a strong black woman, did not ask for our opinion when it came to college; we had no choice. Her father graduated from New York University and Columbia University in the early 1900s. Her mother graduated from Shaw University in the 20s. My mom's twin, Dr. Jacquelyne J. Jackson, was the first tenured African-American female professor at Duke University. The only option I had was college. While I was in the Army, I learned life's greatest lesson: don't repeat mistakes of the past. Even though I was enlisted, I earned rank fast. However, I repeated the same mistake as my father, alcoholism. One sergeant in Germany told me that when I was sober I was the best person in the world, but when I drank, "all hell breaks loose." After my second tour in Germany and the birth of my oldest child, I realized I had a problem. I called my mom during one of my drinking binges and something snapped inside of me. It said, "You are acting just like your dad!" That was a sobering moment for me. It took another couple of years for me to stop drinking completely.

My family transferred to Key West, and I eventually divorced my first wife and got married to my second wife. My second wife and I birthed two wonderful children. I have a total of three outstanding and beautiful children. Unfortunately, after 18 years of marriage, in 2014, we divorced. This was a very difficult time period for me.

Before my divorce, I contracted a viral infection the day before Father's Day in June 2013 that caused me to lose the use of my legs. I was admitted to the Kennestone Hospital in July where I underwent open-heart surgery to replace my aortic and mitral heart valve. My aortic arch was rebuilt. In October 2013 my heart function declined again, and I was rushed back to the hospital to have a pacemaker implanted inside my chest. God is good! That December my mom passed at age 83 in Topeka, Kansas. The following April my ex asked for a divorce. The divorce was finalized that following December.

Since I am a self-employed telecommunications consultant, my business suffered. For the majority of 2014, I earned no income. I was forced to apply for public assistance to take care of my children. But I knew that is not where God wanted me to stay. I was granted full custody of my children for I knew that God was not done with me. I know it is important for both parents to be active participants in their child's life, but if the parents can't stay together it is important for both to be involved. I decided I was not going to be an absent father. So, I made a sacrifice for my children (especially my daughter). It is just as important for fathers to be involved as mothers. It is important for both parents to commit to God first, then each other. I've learned that the hard way. There have been a lot of bumps and a bruises along the way, but just like a diamond character is shaped by cutting and polishing, so is mine. I am trying my best to be an example of a dedicated servant to God and a steady hand to my children.

It is my prayer that God will bring my helpmate. I've been seeking and who knows, maybe He already has. Seek God first; everything else will fall into place.

> *Greatness is not measured by what a man or woman accomplishes, but by the opposition he or she has overcome to reach his goals.*
>
> DOROTHY HEIGHT

A PRAYING WOMAN OF GOD

SELENA PEOPLES

As a mother of three, I always prayed that I would be able to leave my children a legacy. I want to be like Lois and Eunice in the Bible. In 2 Timothy 1:5, the Bible shows us that Paul described Lois and Eunice as having sincere faith passed down throughout the generations of their family. To be found faithful in prayer is a life goal I have set. I plan to pass this legacy on to my children.

Leaving a legacy worth remembering requires staying close to God. We must literally abide in Him. I want my children to love the Lord. I want them to stay close to and abide in Him always. I want them to love the Lord with all their heart, soul and mind. And I want them to use their strength to love their neighbors as themselves as stated in Matthew 22:38.

God wants us to become a student of His Word and be faithful in our prayer life. We must remain pure and holy for He is holy. And we should guard are heart and mind against sin. Life is short but our legacy lasts for eternity. What you do in this life will impact generations to come. I can honestly say without a doubt that my parents left me with the legacy of prayer and love. I grew up in a home where we said the words, "I love you" all the time. Because of the words that were spoken in my home, it's easy for me to receive and understand God's love. My parents were always good to me even when I made a mistake or did something wrong.

To understand how prayer works, let me give you an illustration. My parents started praying in the mornings out loud. I believed the reason they prayed out loud was to get our attention. It was so loud that they woke everyone in the house. I would listen to them and wish I could pray to God the way they did. One morning, I patiently waited for my parents to come out of their bedroom. I said slowly in a trembling voice, "God is not hard of hearing." My parents responded, "He's not nervous either!" Immediately, they sat me down and showed me what the Bible said about prayer. I was forever changed by what I learned. After that, I began to spend time praying and reading the Bible with my parents.

Mom and dad had me read John 17:13. They explained to me that Jesus prayed out loud so that those who heard Him could know joy in Him. We also read, Hebrews 10:19-22. Their explanation of that scripture grounded me and helped me know how to abide more in God. I learned that praising God and declaring truth in prayer about Him assures us of our salvation. I learned that asking God for His help out loud is a way that we can draw near to Him. I learned that praying out loud is a way to encourage one another to love and do God's work.

My parents truly left me with the legacy of prayer. Often I rise at 4:00 a.m. I pray hard and loud and awake everyone in my house just like my parents did. Throughout the years, I have learned more about the importance of praying the Word to overcome spiritual resistance to God's plan for my life. The Holy Spirit has helped me understand so many scriptures and how to use them in prayer.

In our faith walk, there is a key to seeing miracles and breakthroughs on a consistent basis. The key is to keep the Word of God which is the, "Word of Faith" in our mouth and heart. The mouth and heart are connected. Luke 6:45 states, "A good man out of the good treasure of his heart brings forth good; and an evil man out of the evil treasure of his heart brings forth evil. For out of the abundance of the heart his mouth speaks." Beloved, God watches over His Word to perform it. Let His promises in His Word, motivate you to always pray. As I continue to pray and confess the Word of God, I continue to pray for and experience the power of God. My communication with God is similar to talking on a phone line, as the lines are always open. He wants us to be in constant communication with Him.

I challenge and encourage my sons, daughter, grandsons, granddaughters, family and generations to come, to call upon the Lord and to spend more time with Him in prayer. Getting to know Him is the most amazing thing. I believe blessings are a result of spending the right amount of time praying, praising and worshiping. It's also important to exercise your faith and do good works. My prayer is that my family and others will see my heart for prayer and experience the results of my prayers too.

I love you to life!

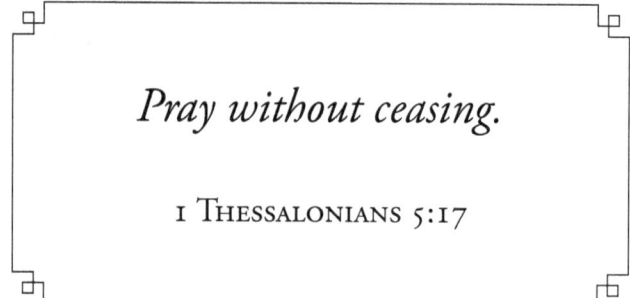

Pray without ceasing.

1 THESSALONIANS 5:17

ATTITUDE MAKES A DIFFERENCE

PRISCILLA WYNN PETERS

It was summer of 1971. Richard Milhouse Nixon was the president at the time. Economically, my family operated with modest means. My daddy was a former Military Army Private who served in the Korean War. After returning home, he found work with Associated Grocers as a truck driver, and he drove a taxi cab part time. My mother was unemployed. She suffered with a liver disorder, yellow jaundice. Daddy did the best he could to provide for me, my mother, and my three sisters. Life was not always easy and resources were often scarce.

It was the, "Age of Aquarius!" My schoolmates wore the latest fashions and often showcased the newest and most popular hairstyles including afros and press and curls. This was their reality; however, it was not mine. My three sisters and I shared a room and bed. Two of us slept at the top and two at the bottom. Often times, I passed my clothes down to whichever sister could fit them. We got by with just enough. The luxuries that others were afforded were not afforded to us, whether it was summer activities, summer camps or just the simple things in life. Those things never added up in our equation. We were overqualified for public assistance and under resourced for everyday living. I wanted to attend Upward Bound, a summer program for underprivileged youth. I got the biggest, "No," I ever received in life. Never again would I accept, "No," for an answer! "Can't," would never be a part of my vocabulary again. My life would never be the same.

I decided that rejection, due to my current state of socioeconomic existence, would not deter me from anything ever again in life. The summer of 1971 taught me valuable lessons. I was determined that I would not miss my opportunity the next summer. My employment application was one of the first in the pile. It was first come, first served. Most outdoor positions were filled, but thank God, there was one more left, cleaning teapots at the

Bobby Dobb Rehabilitation Facility for disabled young adults. It was a dirty job, but it helped me develop a beautiful character.

This facility was like one I never seen before, and there was only one familiar face. She was a girl I befriended in the community. We often played on the playground together. We were unprepared for the job we were tasked with. We were given more than 200 pots daily to clean and scrub. Obviously, my friend and I had never done anything like that before. Who knew teapots could be so beautiful on the outside, but after use, so difficult to clean? Well, my friend complained, played and failed to clean the pots well. She hated the very thought of coming to work. I know you're wondering why I mentioned her pessimism regarding our job. Washing tea pots was hard work. It involved lots of sweat dripping from my face, but my attitude was that of gratitude. I wanted to scrub the pots and clean them to the best of my ability. I didn't like doing it, but I knew I only was doing it for a few days of my summer. Facing many challenges, obstacles and difficult tasks with humility and a great attitude made a difference.

Washing teapots that summer helped me to clearly see the difference between me and my friend. I realized my attitude was nothing like hers. Sarah's pessimism taught me optimism. I worked hard, and at the end of the summer my boss awarded me with a Certificate of Appreciation for a job well done.

In 2015, 45 years later, who would have ever thought I would meet that same boss again? I ran into him at a fundraiser for a local college. He remembered that place of employment. We hugged, laughed and took a walk down memory lane. If he would have remembered me to have a bad attitude, our encounter wouldn't have been pleasant. When he asked about Sarah and if I knew what became of her, I wasn't sure. I think she married after high school, but I wasn't certain what career path she took. However, despite her attitude toward working, I thank God for helping me early in life to accept a difficult assignment with a great attitude.

Being the oldest sibling I've always had the most responsibilities around the house. My dad always made me do chores. For example, I had to do yard work, cook, clean the house and wash clothes. Because we didn't have a dryer, we hung the clothes on a clothesline outside. The chores I hated most were emptying, washing and hanging my younger sibling's diapers. So, in comparison, washing teapots was not difficult. Mama always said, "Pay your own way and don't depend on anyone to take care of you. You need your own money. Don't look for us to give or loan you money all the time. Make your own way!" One day my dad took me in the room and closed the door. He sat me down and said, "Let's get this out of your mind right now! Nothing is free. I don't want you to grow up thinking things are free or you can get something for nothing!" I came out with tears in my eyes and a little sense in my head. My parents taught me how to work hard and be self-sufficient.

That summer, I developed an important character trait that would carry me throughout life. The Bible says, in 2 Peter 1:3, "According as His divine power hath given unto us all things that pertain unto life and godliness through the knowledge of him that hath called us to glory and virtue." Per Colossians 3:22-25 MSG, "Servants do what you're told by your earthly masters. And don't just do the minimum that will get you by; Do your best. Work from the heart for your real master. For God, confident that you'll get paid in full when you come into your inheritance. Keep in mind always that the ultimate Master you're serving is Christ; the sullen servant who does shoddy work will be held responsible."

These scriptures are what I strive to live by. I want my children, their children and future generations to carry this with them in the confines of their hearts. The words of the scripture are not void. Your attitude always determines your altitude!

MY MAMA USED TO SAY…BE PREPARED, BE READY AND BE ON TIME!

LAMAR REED

I am the oldest of five children. I have four sisters. Many years ago before I got my driver's license, my father and mother were the only two drivers in the family. My father was a laid back person. My mother was a stickler about being on time. We had to be on time for dinner. We had to be on time for school. We had to have our homework done and turned in on time. And we had to be on time coming in the house before it got dark.

We had to prepare for church on Saturday night because we had to be on time for church on Sunday morning. I remember my mama saying: "Be ready and be on time when I am ready to pull out of the drive way leaving for church. If you are not ready, you will get left behind and dealt with when I return." My mother would dress my two younger sisters first then she would get dressed. Me and my older sister would get dressed and wait for my mother near the front door. My other sister was always the slower one to get dressed. I remember her not being ready to go and being left behind on many occasions. She would end up staying home with my father who at the time did not attend church. I am grateful to my mother for instilling in us at an early age how important it is to be prepared, be ready and to always be on time. She truly prepared me and my sisters for the different challenges we would face as we got older.

I was drafted in the U.S. Army during the Vietnam War era and retired after serving 30 years. My first 8 weeks of Army boot camp was not hard for me to adjust like some of the other soldiers. The first thing you learn as a soldier in military boot camp is to be prepared, be ready and be on time. Because when the mission calls – one must be alert to go into action. When my three sons were growing up, I always told them what my mother told me. Now I hear my sons telling their kids to: *be prepared, be ready and be on time!*

TIED UP, TANGLED UP, AND TURNED LOOSE

VERA REED

If I had to do my life all over, I would choose to not have sex out of wedlock. Even though I grew up in a Christian home, it was hard for me as a teenager. My parents didn't let me associate with friends at school including boys. However, they allowed me to have friends at church. My parents had five children, three boys and two girls. As the oldest, my responsibility was to keep the house clean and wash the dishes. At school, girls talked about boys and partying. My father and mother told me boys were bad and to not befriend them. Of course, I didn't believe that and still desired to have a boyfriend. But, I obeyed my parents and stayed away from them. Naturally, boys did not bother me because they knew I had three brothers.

My senior year in high school was exciting yet disappointing at times. Prom was approaching, and I wanted to attend. I gained enough courage to ask my parents for permission to attend, and naturally, they were against it. I was determined; I could not miss this event. So, my baby brother persuaded dad and mom to let me go to the prom with him as my date. As we walked in the gym, we noticed the expressions on the students' faces. Students were talking loud, and I could hear them say, "Vera couldn't get a date so she brought her brother." At times, peers can be mean and cruel. At that moment I felt hurt, so we stayed for only an hour.

My father was old school. He saved money for my brothers to go to college. He stated that my sister and I could get husbands to take care of us. However, after graduation I applied for several job positions. I wanted a civil service job in the Federal Government. Finally I acquired a job through a temporary work agency as a supply clerk at Ginn's Office Supply Company.

In September 1967, I accepted a position as a part-time rating clerk at U.S. Civil Commission, now known as the Office of Personnel Management (OPM). I enjoyed working at OPM and I met many people. I felt alive and was happy to be a part of the Federal Family. There was a group of us who ate lunch together every day. In my department, I became friends with a male associate. I felt very comfortable around him. I enjoyed his company until he began making sexual advances. At first his verbal sexual advances felt good but then he wanted more. For several months, I resisted the temptation and refused to have sex with him, so he distanced himself.

I tried to hold out, but I couldn't handle not being with him. Being inexperienced and naive in a relationship, I asked him to teach me. Long story short, I became pregnant. I tried to hide my pregnancy from my parents, but my mother knew. She was furious.

In my seventh month, I gave birth to a baby boy. My mom disconnected from me; however, my dad embraced and forgave me. My dad and his mother made arrangements for us to get married. Can you say, "Big mistake?" My marriage only lasted six months, and it was holy hell. That man didn't allow me to go to church. He wanted a subservient wife to take care of the baby, cook, and to starch and iron his shirts. He would abuse me if I didn't satisfy his sexual needs. Our finances were jacked up, so I took on a part-time job. Just when I thought things were getting better between us, all hell broke loose. I was at work when I received a call from the hospital nurse informing me that my husband was ready to be picked up. At that time I didn't know the reason he was there. When I arrived at the hospital, I was informed that he was being treated for a venereal disease. While being treated he had an allergic reaction to the medicine and passed out. On the cab ride home, he didn't say a word. Once we got home, he had the audacity to blame me for his condition. I was livid and we argued all night. I could not stay in that house any longer, so I left to stay with his mother around the corner. He and his mother didn't have a good relationship, so I really didn't want to get her involved with our problems. He always disrespected his mother. I was so hurt, because I worked so hard in our marriage. I got my own place, and we started dating again. I loved him and thought we would get back together.

After a couple of dates, I found out that he was intimate with someone else whose name happened to be Vera too. That's when I filed for divorce. I was determined I would not get married again. However, God had a plan and purpose for my life. After 15 years of waiting, God blessed me with a good, fine, loving, supportive and God-fearing husband of 31 years whom I love dearly. I went back to school and obtained a B.A. Degree in Marketing at St. Leo University. And I received certification from the Institute for Integrated Nutrition in New York. Presently, I am studying Chinese medicine in a Master Health Coach Program. Also, I am a Certified Health Coach and a Wellness Practitioner.

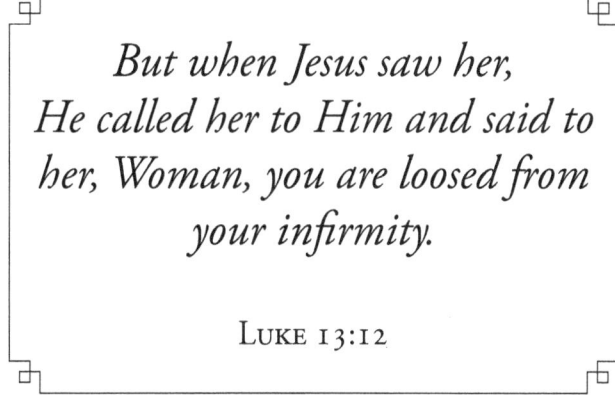

But when Jesus saw her, He called her to Him and said to her, Woman, you are loosed from your infirmity.

LUKE 13:12

WHATEVER YOU DO--DON'T LOSE YOUR PRAISE

THELMA RIGBY

I love to praise God. Praising God is one of the most effective ways to enter into His presence. Praising God has been a God-given weapon that has helped sustain me over the years. Praising God is my testament that hope is alive. And where there is hope, there is faith and where there is faith, all things are possible with God.

Whether in a song or dance of praise, the Lord knows I enjoy giving Him praise. I've always found strength in praising God. It seems as though I praise Him more during times of adversity. It confuses the devil when we praise God during adversities. So, instead of crying and complaining, I get my praise on and things seem to work out.

Praise allows us to become intimate with God and gives us the opportunity to show appreciation for all that He has done for us. When we show our appreciation, we are able to build a foundation of hope. When I praise God, I focus entirely on Him. I praise Him for what He's done for me and who He is. Then I am ushered into a place of worship. Worship is the intimacy I live for because during times of worship, God speaks to me and brings forth healing, restoration and peace to my spirit. My intimacy with God, allows me to rest and know that He is everything I need and more.

He is my Jehovah Jireh, my provider; Jehovah Shalom, my peace; and Jehovah Rapha, my healer. There has never been a time in my life that God has not come through. Now, that doesn't mean He has always said, "Yes" to every request made. It doesn't mean that situations have always resolved in the manner in which I hoped and prayed for, but it simply means that I know that He knows what's best for me. Although I don't always understand the process when I'm going through it, God always works things out for my good. Just thinking about His favor, grace and protection over me, in spite of my mistakes causes praise down in my soul to rise up and give God glory.

As a young saint, I didn't' understand, 2 Corinthians 12:10: "Therefore I take pleasure in infirmities, in reproaches, in needs, in persecutions, in distresses, for Christ's sake. For when I am weak, then I am strong." Over the course of my walk with God, I've come to understand that it is when I am the weakest, I should rely upon God the most. And during those times, He shows up in my life, in a mighty way. Sometimes in my quiet time, I think about my life. I think about the victories, the challenges, the disappointments and what He has promised me in His Word. I weep because I know without God, I am nothing but with God, the sky is the limit.

My great grandparents who had limited monetary resources but a very strong faith in God raised me. Their example was very instrumental in the development of my faith. I grew up believing that with God, all things are possible. I believe that if I can think it, with the help of God, I can do it. I give God the glory for all that He has done in my life. When I think about the goodness of Jesus and all He's done for me, my soul cries Hallelujah! I thank God for saving me. Just knowing where He brought me from and remembering my triumphs and victories gives me hope that the latter will be greater!

> *Then he said to them, "Go your way, eat the fat, drink the sweet, and send portions to those for whom nothing is prepared; for this day is holy to our Lord. Do not sorrow, for the joy of the LORD is your strength.*
>
> NEHEMIAH 8:10

GRADUATION DREAM COME TRUE

JACQUELINE SIMS

In 1969 I graduated High School and was so excited because I was headed to Paine College in Augusta, Georgia. It was going to be my first time away from home with my friends and freedom. Before I left for college my life took an unexpected turn. My mother's husband left her pregnant with twins. After the delivery of the twins, my mother became ill and I was the only one to care for her.

At seventeen I immediately assumed the role as a caretaker for mom and became a mom and dad to my twin brothers. Instead of leaving for college – I took a full time job at Blue Cross and Blue Shield Insurance Co. and became the head of the household.

Eventually my grandmother came to live with us to help out with my mom and brothers. I began to get excited again about college and enrolled in Georgia State University using my company's education benefits to pay my tuition. But that was short lived as I had to withdraw to help out at home.

I worked 12 years and decided to give college a try again. I enrolled in Spelman College at the age of 47. Most people thought I was crazy. Back then it was not that popular for more mature people to go back to school. I didn't let what others say deter me because there was a dream in my heart that just would not die.

Like Joseph in the Bible, God had birthed a dream in his heart that could not be quenched. Joseph had to endure betrayal by his brothers, enslavement, imprisonment, more betrayal, false accusations from the pharaoh's wife and a host of other mishaps. But there is something about a dream. It drives you and it won't let you go. If you yield to your dream it will carry you through any trial.

Dr. Martin Luther King had a dream that he wouldn't let die. It carried him to places that he never imagined. Nelson Mandela had a dream for freedom for his people. Do you think that the path that he was forced to take was something he imagined? The dream or purpose for our lives is placed in our hearts by God almighty. Despite what we may think, we are not placed upon this earth to pursue our own purpose. God says, in Jeremiah 29:11, "For I know the thoughts that I think toward you, saith the LORD, thoughts of peace, and not of evil, to give you an expected end." God has an expected end for our lives and that end is for good.

As we pursue God's divine plan for our lives we will encounter some setbacks, some draw backs, some near failures but God has a plan that includes the entire human race. And each of our lives is designed to fit intricately into His divine plan.

God has placed a dream in your heart. Please seek Him and be willing to change your plans to find God's plan for your life. And as you surrender to His will take heed to the following.

- Protect your mind; be mindful of what you allow to enter your mind
- The battle between good and evil is to see who will control your mind
- Don't compare yourself to others
- Discover your own land and then stay in it
- Only you can become the best you that you can be

I held on to my dream of being a college graduate. It took me 12 years but I graduated from Spelman College at the age of 59. May God bless you and may His Holy Spirit rest, rule and abide with you and may His angels always go before you and protect your way as you pursue the dream He placed in your heart.

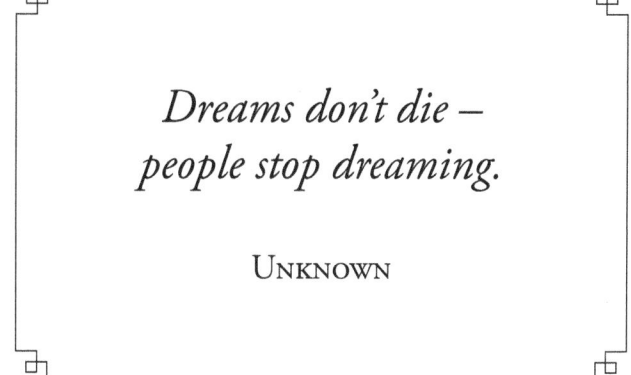

Dreams don't die – people stop dreaming.

UNKNOWN

HOW I MET MYSELF

GREG WAYNE SMITH

For 54 years, I Gregory Wayne Smith lived in a make-believe, self-absorbed fantasy world unbeknownst to me until now. Ironically while writing my story, I came face-to-face with a new creation this week after experiencing a series of life-changing events the summer of 2015 in Atlanta, Georgia. This is so surreal at this precise moment in time. Each new day entails inward introductions much like unraveling an orange to get to the fruit of life. I'll explain this remarkable twist in plot and how it all came together for this new babe in Christ like scattered pieces of a complex jigsaw puzzle.

Born and raised in the projects of Southeast Washington D.C., I spent most of my childhood daydreaming of how I wanted to shape the world around me and live a more prosperous and meaningful life than my parents, George and Nancy. I owe my financial drive and determination to my pops who instilled strong capitalistic views upon me since he missed the mark. At age 10, he made me promise to become self-reliant and to never rely on anyone for anything. His legacy quote was, "It's a dog-eat-dog world out there, so stop barking and leave no crumbs!" I adored my dad; he was called home to heaven much too soon. Years later, I began teaching my main man (my son Gregory Abercrombie Smith), the same ferocious principles.

My transition into manhood started while attending the University of Maryland, College Park. Go Terps! After becoming a proud member of Omega Psi Phi Fraternity, completing my Master's Degree, launching a professional career and watching my bank account grow faster than a pirate's beard, I arrived! According to Proverbs 23:7, "You become what you think." I often described myself as hard working, ambitious, success driven, dedicated worker, never late and a team player, but not one mention of my soul or spirit man. I guess I was just too busy ignoring God and searching for happiness. I was a world traveler, bass guitarist, drummer, certified scuba diver, snow boarder, kayaker, surfer, water boarder, small plane pilot, sky diver, table tennis player, motorcyclist, long distance bicyclist, painter, sculptor and the list continues. Something was missing! Although 'stuff' made me happy, it had no staying power, so I shifted my focus to women. Several failed relationships later, I was still unable to reach that carrot. Happiness didn't seem so elusive with a faster sports car, bigger crib, awesome job and more money than I could count. But still something was missing.

I felt empty. Where is the love? Heck, I achieved in 20 years what most men would not amass in two lifetimes; even Popeye in a spinach patch couldn't maintain my pace. Chest puffed out and thinking I arrived, I still wanted to pour more things down that black-holed soul. Reaching that mid-century mark made life unbearable. With both parents deceased, failed relationships and forced to spend endless quiet nights alone, God found me! First He directed me to a church within walking distance, then I found my mom's old Bible layered in dust.

Ezekiel 36:26 states, "God will replace our hearts of stone with a brand new one carved from love." In January 2013, I reconnected with my wife, Teresa 'Tee' Charles-Smith in miraculous fashion and moved all of my worldly possessions south on a midnight train. Finally, this is the castle I saw in third grade, the vehicles I sketched in fifth grade, the love I aspired since being a college junior and the corporate position my Pops molded me for before unleashing me in that smelly dog pound. What now? I found my thrill! So what was lacking?

Intellectually I knew what was missing, a true relationship with God – My God, not my mom's, not Tee's God, but just me and the creator of Heaven and Earth. My obstacle was that I didn't want or know how to sacrifice life's most precious gift –

my time. Traveling through my universe at warp speeds, I barely found time to think let alone for prayer, meditation or character building. Then one rainy autumn morning in 2014, my spiritual voyage began when I saw Bishop Dale C. Bronner on TV preaching on the, "Passion of Life" series. I dropped everything, went on the internet, purchased the teachings and immediately started attending the Word of Faith Family Worship Cathedral (WOF) after returning from my Christmas vacation in Australia. Still, now what?

I knew it, could feel it, but could not describe it to others, so I kept this sense of emptiness internal. Suddenly, in the still of the day while sitting near our lake and watching five hummingbirds play tag, my entire universe shifted. Both my wife and I were jobless with no money streams. Mentally paralyzed and physically drained by no job and a nearly negative bank account, I quickly became engrossed with unimaginable fear of financial ruin, losing stuff and simply not knowing God's plan. My knees buckled as if I was in a heavyweight championship bout with four lions. Tee remained a pillar of faith. She had a 30-year relationship with Jesus Christ, but her endless faith was still not enough for me. I stood motionless, or better yet powerless, in the eye of the storm. Life's answer came when I looked in the mirror through crocodile tears and saw no reflection. I was missing.

Thank God for the WOF Men's Ministry, Bishop's spiritual instructions, my Bible and most of all Tee's patience, unconditional love, selflessness, saintly wisdom and righteous living. For the first time ever, I heard the Holy Spirit's voice. He said, "Welcome and say hello to you! You are simply my child. No other titles matter. Continue to follow me. Your path is set. You are equipped. No more fear. No fear." I called my son, Greg, that day and shared my story and vision. He responded, "Pops, I saw the change the day you accepted Christ as your Lord and Savior. I'm glad you see it now!"

Today I'm spirit-led, a cheerful giver, a strong father, fun, spontaneous, compassionate, faith-seeking, God-fearing, kindhearted and a loving husband. Greg is our legacy. My focus is not on what God can do for me or finding that dream job or accumulating more stuff but how I can best serve others, increase God's Kingdom, love more and empower generations to come. Tee once wrote to me, "I could see into you, the boy who wanted to be free to develop and mature into the mighty prosperous man of God you were meant to be. No matter who or what, stay with the Lord. He will never leave you nor forsake you. Place Him first and everything else will align according to His plan and purpose for your life. I'm a living witness. So hello Gregory, go forth and prosper in the things of God. He has great things for you. You can trust in Him, because He is faithful. He has begun a great work in you, so walk with Him. I'll be with you my friend, even beyond the end!"

Wow! Not once did my phone ring, email chime or conference call demand my attention while reflecting on what really mattered at that moment. Paul the Apostle reminded us in 1 Thessalonians 5:18 to give God thanks for everything, especially His will in our lives. The only things that have changed are my faith, attitude and passion for my future. My message is simple, "Look for God, not stuff, to fill life's void and find that missing piece to your puzzle!" I'm enjoying my season of rest, and I love that great guy God introduced me to this week.

> *You have to leave the city of your comfort and go into the wilderness of your intuition. What you'll discover will be wonderful. What you'll discover is yourself.*
>
> — ALAN ALDA

LIFELONG LEARNING: POWER TWINS OF TRUSTING AND TITHING

TERESA CHARLES-SMITH

Trust in the Lord with all your heart and lean not on your own understanding; in all your ways acknowledge him and he will make your paths straight (Proverbs 3:5-6).

The Lord commands us to trust Him. There are benefits for trusting Him. Here are a few: salvation through His son Jesus, deliverance, discernment, favor, finances, forgiveness, grace, health, healing, love, peace, protection, provision, sound mind, super natural interventions, wisdom, wealth, zoe life and so much more. The list could continue because He is an infinite God. Every believer has a personal testimony of how the Lord has manifested His promises in their life. If you are a believer, you trusted Him by faith to receive His plan of salvation. I first trusted Him with my life when I accepted Jesus as my personal Savior. I asked Him to use my life for His glory. I asked Him to help me navigate through life so I can enjoy it in abundance. Also I asked Him to lead me into eternity with Him at the appointed time. Life in Christ, for me, has never been a dull moment. He keeps on proving Himself to me. I live by the tithing principle of God's Word in Malachi 3.

Let me share about trusting in the Lord in the area of tithing. Tithing is one of my favorite areas of God's plan that I enjoy talking about. I realize it is a sensitive subject for some and maybe of no interest to others. Sisters and brothers, tithing connects you to God's covenant promises, opens the windows of heaven, pours out blessing on your life like a full pitcher of water – so much, you won't have room enough to receive. The devourer, the one who steals, kills and destroys is rebuked, stopped for your sake and my sake and everyone who will get involved.

A tithe is 10 percent of your earnings. Anything under or over 10 percent is an offering. Fear not, this is God's A+ rated divine financial plan. His plan takes care of His house and your house simultaneously. In many cases, 90 percent may be enough to meet your daily needs but never enough to meet your needs in the unseen realm or your desires. He said He would give us the desires of our heart. How amazing what His 'super' on our 'natural' can do. Here is the formula:

10% to God + 90% for us (to manage wisely of course) = uncommon multiplicity.

Imagine this, serving in your calling, fulfillment in career, contentment in marriage and relationships, world-wide travel, Godly houses, debt-free cars, debt-free education, discounts, freebies, fine dining, favor-favor-favor, lending and not borrowing, gift giving, seed sowing, healings, miracles, provisions during under employment and no employment. Imagine having access to accrued benefits stored until needed like unexpected income. Imagine preventing misfortune in the lives of others, sharing, investing, owning and increasing more and more; all from 10 percent of a teacher's salary. No other explanation, but God. You can now see how the tithe activates the supernatural and positions you to receive the desires of your heart. Tithing has always been my first step of personal financial management. I often tell others I can't afford not to tithe, it provides my lifestyle. I need His system to remain active at all times in every area of my life.

Activate the supernatural system over your life. Return to God what belongs to Him, Give your tithes to your local church and watch Him pour out on your life. Trust Him, prove Him and prosper.

> *And all the tithe of the land, whether of the seed of the land or of the fruit of the tree, is the Lord's. It is holy to the Lord.*
>
> LEVITICUS 27:30

THE INSTRUCTIONS I FOLLOW DETERMINES THE FUTURE I CREATE

THELMA TALLEY

The instructions I follow determine the future I create. Ultimately, I am responsible for what I say and do, thus I choose to be patient.

This is a lesson I want you to know: Life has a way of unfolding according to God's timetable not yours. Therefore, life requires a great amount of patience. When I find my patience tested to the limit, I slow down and trust God. God may say wait but He never says worry.

My weaknesses, faults, fears and insecurities were not strong enough to wound God's Word. Scriptures in the Bible are words of truth and quickens the Holy Spirit within me. The scriptures allow me to wait, hope and expect God's good for me.

After 32 years of marriage and three sons, Quintin, Jerome and Reginald, my husband (their father) passed March 3, 1990. He left me alone after being with him all those years. I survived the loss of a loved one by being patient and believing in God's Word. Hebrew 4:12 is one of my favorite scriptures. I read it during my quiet time every morning.

The Word of God has supernatural effects when I receive it by faith. I read it, meditate on it, believe it and apply it to my life. When I read God's Word in Hebrew 4:12, I realized that God doesn't speak just to hear His own voice. He speaks to be heard. As a believer my destiny is not to live in fear and defeat but to live in victory.

Beloved, I want you to know how I learned patience. I learned patience through trusting God at his Word, which helped me survive the loss of a loved one. You can overcome many obstacles by applying patience and having expectancy that God is working it out for your good His Word says so.

Thelma Talley

Now may the Lord direct your hearts into the love of God and into the patience of Christ.

2 THESSALONIANS 3:5

RAIN, PAIN AND RAINBOWS

LINDA TAYLOR

Prior to July 18, 1979, I lived a wonderful life. God blessed me with a wonderful husband and three beautiful children. My husband was employed at General Motors. We owned a nice home, two cars and a motor home. We traveled every chance we could get and we took the children to Panama City, Florida, every spring break. My mother and father often traveled with us. We were Atlanta Falcons season ticket holders and we would even take the children with us to New Orleans for the Falcons game. Wherever we traveled they traveled with us. We went to church on Sundays. The children were in the children's choir, and I was one of the lead singers in the gospel chorus. The gospel chorus would travel as far as New York City and Washington, D.C.

One summer Day in 1979, we planned a cook out at Adams Park in Atlanta, Georgia. My mom, dad, best girlfriend, and the children were to meet my husband and some friends once they finished work around 4 p.m. All was going well. The hot dogs and burgers were grilling and the children were playing while we all sat talking and having fun. Suddenly a heavy dark cloud seemed to appear out of no where. There were severe lightning flashes and loud thunder clashes. We never had a chance to finish cooking. We were surrounded by trees and very sharp lightning flashes.

As we were rushing to gather our things and get to our vehicles, my husband was stretched out on a chaise, laughingly saying, "Why are y'all rushing? Don't you know God will take care of you?" We hurriedly got into our cars, and my 14-year-old daughter rolled down the window and said to my daddy, "Be careful Daddy." All of the grandchildren called our daddy, "Daddy." Rain

began to fall by the bucketful and huge balls of hail fell with the rain. It was a terrible summer storm.

Once we reached I-285 West, the rain was blinding and traffic had slowed to about 15 to 20 mph. On top of the storm, it was rush hour traffic, so the expressway was full. My 11-year-old son was in the front seat and had fallen asleep with his head in my lap as my husband drove. I looked back at my girls, ages 14 and 15, as my 14-year-old was shivering. I asked if she was cold, she replied, "Yes," so I asked my husband to lower the air fan. Just as I turned around my daughter yelled, "Look at that car!" I looked on the opposite of the expressway of 1285 E, and I exclaimed "Look at that truck!" A white Cadillac had cut short in front of an 18-wheeler with a red cab, and he clipped the car causing it to fishtail. The truck driver lost control of the truck causing it to careen across the median head on into our station wagon, instantly killing my husband and 14-year-old daughter who was sitting directly behind him.

Once the cab hit our vehicle, I heard a rumbling sound, I looked to my left and though it was very cloudy and raining very hard, I saw a blinding bright light on the trailer side of the truck. I remember screaming "Lord we're all going to die!"

At that point I felt a euphoric type of feeling as if I was wondering where I was. I came to what seemed to be a V-shaped road. The left side was a dark tunnel with an extremely bright light, and the right side was bright hazy looking daylight. I was drawn to the left side. As I approached, I saw a field of tall grass that looked more like wheat and flowers sticking up taller than the grass. As I moved further, I wasn't taking steps; I seemed to be floating instead. I came upon a very narrow stream and was stopped by an unseen force. After making two or three attempts, (all the while wondering what was holding me back from stepping over that stream) I looked up and saw my daughter on the other side. At the cook-out, my daughter had on jeans and a burgundy t-shirt.

My daughter was standing against a three-rail white picket fence. Her arms stretched out along the top rail and one foot was propped up on the bottom rail, she had on a white dress, and she was smiling. We communicated without a sound. I understood her and she understood me. I wanted to know why I couldn't cross that stream and get to where she was, and she was saying to me that I could not come. She never said why.

My attention was diverted by a voice calling out to me, "Hello, can you hear me?" Then I heard someone say, "She's coming around, she's alive!" I opened my eyes and I saw emergency vehicles, the first one I saw was a fire truck and I wondered if our vehicle was on fire or about to explode. My son's head was still lying in my lap, and he asked me if he could get up. I told him not to move and just lay where he was. I remember scooping up a handful of coagulated blood from a wound in his head. A lady with a black umbrella came up and peeked over at my husband and immediately shrieked "Oh my God!" I later learned that my husband had been decapitated. My 14-year-old daughter, who was sitting directly behind my husband was deceased also. The death certificate said it was a blunt force trauma. Someone stopped my 15-year-old daughter who was running down the expressway screaming for help, she thought we were all dead. They carried her to South Fulton Hospital, my son and I was taken to Holy Family Hospital, and the two bodies of my loved ones were taken to Grady.

My life was over… I wished so badly that I had died in that accident. I know it sounds selfish. My mother told me I still had to live for my two other children, I just didn't see how I could possibly go on. I was so angry with God. The pastor said at the funeral that God does not plan these thing to happen, however he allows them to happen for reasons of His own. That was very little consolation to me. I had never known hurt, pain and heartache like I was experiencing. I couldn't eat or sleep, but I tried my best to be there for my children. I vowed that I would never marry again, and I just didn't know how I was going to carry on.

My husband did everything for me, and now I had to wing it on my own. I was a wreck for quite some time because I was wrestling with my emotions. One day I was sad and another day I was angry. I would mourn my lost loved ones then I would mourn for my remaining two children having to live a life without their sister and father, then I would mourn for myself having to live a life without them, and then I would vent my anger to God. How could I consider Him a God of love when He allowed something so cruel to happen to me? I went to church, I was taught that the family that prays together stays together. And now, look at what I was facing? My husband was a good husband and father, my own mother and father thought the world of him, and if he had any enemies they were unknown to him. He had a very outgoing personality, met no strangers, and everyone who knew him was a friend to him and vice versa. My daughter was just as sweet as they come. Her dream was to become an attorney. I went on this way for quite some time. I would see my children off to school, and I would spend the remainder of the day crying, crying for them and for myself. My anger at God began to cease, and I realized that He had never left me, that he was right beside me the entire time. I never stopped communicating with Him, though I talked so much that I never slowed down to realize He had been speaking to me all along. One particular day I stopped to listen, and He told me how much He loved me and not to worry. He said everything was going to be all-right if I just let Him carry me, and that is the day that I chose to do so.

I can't begin to tell you what it is like to be carried by God. I say God, but when He spoke to me He said, "Jesus loves you more than you can ever imagine." There are no words known to me to describe what it feels like to have Him carry me. That day was the beginning of the rest of my life. I had a friend who loved and cared about my every pain. I would talk with Him all day, every day until He started to put me down to walk. I told Him, "No, I am not ready," and He said, "Yes, you are, you're stronger than you think you are."

I never want that kind of hurt again, however, my relationship with Jesus was worth every second of hurt I felt. I know that He loves me, and He still walks and talks with me every day, and I can feel His closeness. But there is nothing like the feeling I had when I was up in His arms as He carried me.

Three years later, God sent an extraordinary man into my life. Two years after meeting him, we married. He is a perfect husband, perfect father to Dee and Shaun, and perfect grandfather to our grandchildren and three great grandchildren. We have been married 34 years, and I love him with all my heart.

God is awesome, and I found that when you are hurting the most, that is when He is closest to you. Even though you may feel there is no reason to go on, if you trust Him and let Him carry you, He will see you through. God gave me a new life and showed me that my daughter was happy. Although I have questions about why God did not show me my husband, I have learned to trust and obey Him. As stated in Isaiah 41:10, "Fear not, for I am with you; Be not dismayed, for I am your God. I will strengthen you, Yes, I will help you, I will uphold you with My righteous right hand."

And He said to me,
My grace is sufficient for you,
for My strength is made perfect in weakness.
Therefore most gladly
I will rather boast in my infirmities,
that the power of Christ may rest upon me.

2 CORINTHIANS 12:9

NOT MY TIME

PATRICIA TERRY

Patricia W. Terry

My name is Patricia Terry and my childhood nickname is Trixie. I am privileged to share with you some of my childhood experiences with two of the four Black girls that were killed in the bombing of the 16th Street Baptist Church. The bombing took place in Birmingham, Alabama, on September 15, 1963. Cynthia Wesley and Carole Robertson were both 14 years old, but I was 16 years old.

I lived in a quiet, friendly, and a well-to-do neighborhood. Angel Davis was my next door neighbor. However, she was 8 years old, and I was only 3 years of age when my family built our home next door to the Davises. The parents in my neighborhood were principals, school teachers, doctors, nurses, lawyers and construction owners. A few of the neighbors were blue-collar parents who either worked at a plant called TCI or ACIPCO. When a position came available at either of the plants, the news media would go to the plants the next day, because people would actually spend the night in line for an opportunity to apply for a job. Each reputable company was known for providing excellent pay and free health benefits.

Every Sunday the entire neighborhood went to Sunday school and church. It appeared that everyone left home on his or her way to church around the same time. Every Sunday everyone was well dressed as if it were Easter Sunday. On Sundays, we were not allowed to play on the playground, but on late Sunday evenings the kids could go to the movies. However, when we would go to any of the movie theaters, Blacks were only allowed to sit in the balcony (upstairs).

During the summertime, all of the kids in the neighborhood would gather on the playground, which was located next to my house. We would play crocket, ping pong, baseball or build tents with blankets. We also played games: hit the hammer, high or low, spin-the-bottle and my favorite game hide-and-seek. Back in those days, kids would play outside until the sunset.

We were only allowed to play on the weekends and during the summer months (unlike the children of this era). My neighborhood was named, "Dynamite Hill."

One day, I overheard my parents discussing the hours and various shifts that men would have to take in patrolling different locations throughout the neighborhood with shotguns. Of course as a very young child, I had no idea why. I remember constantly peeping out of the window watching the men patrol the neighborhood. I discovered later that Chief of Police Bull Conner, announced on the radio that a Black family moved in on the White side of Center Street, and that there would be bombings and blood shed that night. Attorney Shoals, a Civil Rights Attorney's house was bombed on two occasions. He and his family lived a block away from us. Because of the numerous threats and bombings, our neighborhood was named, "Dynamite Hill."

I met my friend Cynthia one weekend when the Wesley Family cared for her. The Wesleys could not have children, so eventually Cynthia's biological mother agreed to allow them to adopt her. Cynthia came from a large family that made it difficult for her mother to financially support the family, so her mother saw an opportunity for one of her children to receive a good education and live a better life.

Cynthia's back door faced my parent's backyard which was across a gravel driveway about an acre away from my house. Cynthia would cut across our yard as a short cut to school. Her dresses were always starched, and her hair ribbons and socks would always match her attire. Cynthia was a thin, fragile looking girl with long pigtails. She always had a big smile on her face. We played together almost every day especially during the summer.

On September 1, 1963, I celebrated my 16th birthday. At that time, Cynthia was only 14 years of age. Usually on Sunday mornings, my mother's cousin, J.L. Lowe, would pick me up and then go around the corner to pick Cynthia up. We would go to the 16th Street Baptist Church where Cynthia played in the band. Usually, the girl band members changed into their band uniforms in the bathroom located in the church basement. The bomb that killed the four girls was planted outside of the basement bathroom. When I joined them, I always found a seat on the front section of the church, so Cynthia and I could make eye contact and giggle about previous conversations.

On the morning of Sunday, September 15, 1963, my mother informed me that I could not go to church with Cynthia because our family church was celebrating its anniversary. I begged my mom to let me go to church with Cynthia because most of my friends also attended that church. My mom did not give in to my plea. When I returned home that day, I heard the shocking news that 16th Street Baptist Church had been bombed. At the time, I had no idea that my friends Cynthia and Carole were the victims of such a horrible tragedy. I later found out that Cynthia's and the other girls' bodies could not be viewed because of the devastating damages from the bombing.

During the funeral, I sat in the Wesleys' living room. I heard screaming throughout the house. Mrs. Wesley asked my mom to allow me to ride to the funeral in their car along with my other girlfriends. We were all able to sit with the family during the service. I remember sitting across Cynthia's biological mother during the funeral session. Some of her siblings were literally passing out. Three of the four girls' funerals took place at the same time and place, but Carole's funeral was on a later date. Since there were three obituaries, I assumed that was why the cries seemed to echo. To this day, I don't think I've ever experienced such a mournful funeral as this one.

Years later, Angela Davis wrote her autobiography. During the 70s she was well known in the Civil Rights struggle and was labeled a

Communist because of her association with the "Black Liberation Movement." One of the quotes in her autobiography described our neighborhood:

"Time did not cool the anger of the White people who still lived on Dynamite Hill. The White people refused to adapt their lives to the presence of Blacks living next door to them. Every so often, a courageous Black family would move or build a house on the White side of Center Street; and the resentment erupted in explosions and fires. The bombing on Dynamite Hill was so common until, eventually the horror diminished."

I've had many experiences with prejudice, but I see people as individuals. I remember at age 17, my pastor and his wife had to relocate to the northern states because our congregation was African American and back in those days, the Lutheran church would not allow a White pastor to adopt a child while pastoring a Black membership church. I remember the couple being very sad because he was the first minister of the new church, and the membership under his leadership had grown tremendously.

At that stage in life, I know that it was not my appointed time to join my friends who were plucked like roses from the garden of life. I would have definitely been in the basement of the 16th Street Baptist Church with Cynthia and the other young ladies had my mother not persistently told me, "No." If their flowers had not been picked at such an early age, they all would've had a flower bed of roses to give to the world.

> *So teach us to number our days, that we may gain a heart of wisdom.*
>
> PSALM 90:12

YOU DON'T NEED EASY – JUST POSSIBLE

ELLA THOMPSON

I worked in the banking industry for 24 years and eventually, it became time for my annual evaluation. I prepared to ask for a big raise due to the added branches and functions senior management assigned to my job description. I mentioned this to my supervisor, but she said a raise was not possible due to budget constraints. That did not sit well with me given the new workload but it seemed there was nothing I could do about it at the time.

A few weeks later, as I was walking in the hallway, the president commended me on my performance in the acquisition. I took the opportunity to ask if he would consider giving me a raise due to the added functions and long hours. He replied, "I will see what I can do." Shortly after that conversation, I was told by my supervisor that I would receive a small raise and a great annual review. The raise was not what I anticipated, but something was better than nothing, so I thought. It was time for a much-needed vacation, so I took off for a few days.

While on vacation, I received a call from my supervisor stating that the president had been looking for me. She even implied that I appeared to be in trouble due to his eagerness to speak to me. She said he walked to my office twice in one day passing her office without uttering a word. On my first day back from vacation, I walked from my car to my office thinking, "What has happened now?" Before I could sit down comfortably, the president walked in my office. He stated that he needed to speak with me and would like to take me to lunch to discuss the details.

I told him it was my first day back and asked if we could discuss it on site because I had not planned to take a lunch. I needed to catch up on the backlog of work I was facing. He then asked me to take a walk up to the 10th floor. The bank needed more space and he was thinking of renting the 10th floor since the radio station moved out of the building. He stated that we would talk there while looking at the office space. He asked me to meet him there in 10 minutes.

Once the elevators opened, I felt a little eerie. It was more about whether I beat him to the floor and would be there alone. When I saw he was there, I started to speak and make small talk. As we walked down one hallway and went into the first empty office, we talked about my raise. He said that he had spoken to my supervisor and I should be getting the raise soon. I did not indicate to him that I already knew of the raise. I just thanked him for his efforts.

As he walked inside the office I stood in the doorway. I turned and leaned on the molding with one foot inside the office and one foot in the hallway. As he was talking I turned my head for a split second. When I turned back, he grabbed my face and squeezed it very tightly while thrusting his tongue down my throat. I started to gag to the point that I almost vomited. As we tussled, I ended up deep within the office and he was now standing in the doorway. "Why is this happening and how do I get out of this?" I thought as I scanned the room. "Please don't," I cried, "I can't do this." I walked in circles until I realized he was not moving. "I have a boyfriend and I.. I.. I.." I uttered as my mind drew a blank. My hands were in the air as if I was being arrested. I tried to walk past him. He reached up and grabbed my hand and placed it on his private parts as he said, "Are you sure you want to pass this up?" I ran as fast as I could. My heart felt as if it was about to beat out of my chest. I knew then that my life was about to change drastically.

I tried to go back to my office and work, but my office was more glass than wall, so I knew I could not cry without being noticed, so I left and went home. I returned the next day not knowing what I would face. One day led to another without any reactions from him. A month passed, and I realized I was losing composure after my supervisor called me in her office and said, "Ella, what is wrong with you? Since you returned from vacation, you have been acting unlike yourself. Can I help?" I knew she was speaking the truth, because every time I heard his voice coming down the hall, I would duck into another office even if someone was in it then apologize for the interruption. I cried in mid conversation with her as I forgot about our weekly reports which was not in my character.

My thoughts were sketchy and my emotions were high. Yes, I knew I was a mess. I responded by saying that I would tell her eventually. I went back to my office and prepared to go to Human Resources (HR) the following day. I told them what happened and waited for the conclusion. Yes, I waited… waited… and waited some more. What I can tell you is that I heard nothing for months, it was pure torture. The torture started when I began to receive phone calls on my cell phone from a disguised voice saying that I better think before speaking to anyone. I also received hang up calls all day long. One of the callers said, "We know where you live. We like the yellow and purple flowers in the flower bed." "Is this for real?" I thought. This is what mob mentality is about. How could they hate me? At this point I did nothing or said nothing. All I said was, "No." Who are they and will they go further than driving by my home and making threatening phone calls? This was a systematic way to mentally lynch me. This all happened three years after my mother died, so I had no one to confide in. I always believed I was strong with good composure, but I was really breaking down. I cried myself to sleep every night. HR had not responded, and I had not received any calls regarding the resumes I sent out. I was really scared, and it was evident that I could not take this much longer.

The president was more valuable to the bank than I was, so when I put in the sexual harassment complaint, they decided they would take the chance and fire me. Keep in mind that I received a "Christmas bonus," which was not given to everyone, a raise and a good review six months prior.

In the termination meeting I asked the director why HR didn't respond to my sexual harassment claim and she replied, in the presence of my supervisor, that she didn't feel my complaint had any merit. I was floored. I went back to my office to pack my items.

Shortly after I returned to the office, the HR director walked in and said that I had to leave the premises immediately. She stated that she would have my things packed and mailed to me. I replied, "I have been in this office for 14 years and I have a lot of personal items as you can see. I will pack as fast as I can." I was holding a box in my hand. She reached out, and knocked it out of my hands while she screamed "I said leave!" I had not anticipated such hostility but I did anticipate something which is why I placed a recorder in my bra before I went to HR. I pulled it out and told her that I had everything on tape. I also said to her, "It is still on. You can call security to come watch me pack, but if you touch me again, you are going to start a fight that you will not win." She ran out of the office, and I continued to pack.

I was told that they had a corporate meeting with all senior management, and the bank conducted an investigation back 14 years which resulted in a dead end. They also told employees that I left for personal reasons. Several so-called co-workers called me to see if I was okay but they all started the call with similar statements, "If you need someone to confide in, call me and I promise you it would be confidential." I did not hold conversations with any of them. However, there was one person I was sure was a true friend, and I did tell her things like, "He never gave me any indication that he saw me in that manner," and "I am seeking someone professional to talk to." Everything I told her was in the paperwork I received from the bank. I was devastated.

I went to church and fell at the altar. It was as if I was the only one in the building. I don't even remember how I got in the back of the church. They must have carried me out. What I can tell you is, I left it all on the altar.

I still did not have the answers to why the HR director would turn on me and be mean and hateful. I was shocked more so at the behaviors of the HR director than the other officers of the bank. The, "Good Old Boy Syndrome," was back in effect. No one cared about how this single mother would survive. My life had been pulled from under me like a rug. I had a mortgage, a car note, a daughter in college and people really couldn't care less. Not only did he assault me, but he threw my life into a whirlwind of unknowns.

Lord, what do I do with this pain? Why didn't I see this action coming? Will I ever be able to trust my own sense of discernment again?

Things were not easy for me. I fasted and prayed while I dried my tears and picked up my life. It was a long road of trials and tribulations. I broke up with my boyfriend and seven years passed before I could even think of dating again. I didn't ask God for, "easy," just "possible."

One day, as I was lying in my bed feeling alone and sad, I began to hate the president for putting me in such a predicament. "Why me?" I asked. I started to fear the outcome of my life. I wondered if God allowed a man to devastate me beyond repair. The challenge for me was watching my pain turn me into a weak and unforgiving soul, until the voice of God reigned in my ears, "I did not give you the spirit of fear, but of power, love and a sound mind." God reminded me that working at the bank was just geography. He reminded me that what I know, I know, and no one can take that away. It was a refreshing thought. I stopped being afraid of the taunting phone calls and simply changed my number. I even thought about preparing a harassment folder with all the evidence. My thought was, "There are law officers for people who exhibit such behaviors."

My final thoughts that night ended on all the things I could add up in place of the painful things. Yes, add it up Ella, you are still above ground, you did not suffer any physical pain and most importantly, you don't even have to worry about those that sought to hurt you. God has appointed you a task. Carry it out, and walk out of the pain which is really just a memory.

It was then that I knew God was with me all the time. I went on to live my life just as I did prior to the assault. My bills were all paid on time; I ate and continued to be loved by my family and friends. I remained a happy, not bitter, person. I continued to walk as a child of God. He did not leave me nor forsake me in my times of trouble.

At the moment of the assault, I asked myself, "Do you choose your dignity or your job?" One of the two will be gone once you run out of that door. I chose God and my dignity remained intact.

When we as disciples of God are hurting and in pain, we must regroup and find the mental pathway to escape the pain through the Word of God. Once we escape mentally, we can physically walk in peace.

It was not easy, but possible is all I needed.

But He said, the things which are impossible with men are possible with God.

LUKE 18:27

A SHIP NEEDS A SAIL TO STAY AFLOAT

GWEN WALKER

I guess you could say that things started working inside me during my elementary school years. During that time I began to realize I had a great love for God's people. It became very obvious to me. I was pretty much a loner, a lot like a ship without a sail. I knew it was not about me at all. I thought nothing about myself. I did what he required of us, "to love ye one another," as stated in John 13:34, 35. I found deep down joy within myself every time I was able to help someone. It felt so good. It angered and hurt me to hear and see my peers being hurt and treated badly because of how they looked, talked, acted or just because they didn't look like the people they were attracted to. The more joy they got out of mistreating others, the angrier I got. I would befriend, encourage and speak life into them, letting them know that they were loved and that somebody cared. I didn't know the Word at that time to really speak from the Bible, but I believed they didn't either. Oh, it was so rewarding!

Since then, I've continued to help God's people. The revelation of my life was that I was not just helping God's people by caring, loving, encouraging and speaking life into them, but they were also helping me. Every person I loved and cared for became a piece of my new sail. That old ship out in the ocean started to gain a sail. It was growing and starting to hold the wind. The people God blessed me to help have become more pieces to additional sails. You see, God took what He put in me and used it for His good.

My life began to start sailing, and God enlarged my territory. He assigned me to people who needed to be lifted, encouraged and have life spoken into them. I enjoyed seeing people's eyes light up and a smile form on their face when they realize they were still useful to God and loved. The reward is priceless. I am no miracle person. I just let God empower me to do what He desires. My encouragement to everyone who loves the Lord is to:

"Brighten the corner where you are!
Because someone far from harbor may guide
you across the bar,
Brighten the corner where you are."

Just going through the day saying something positive to someone lets them know they matter to God, and He still loves them. In the grocery store, in the bank, at the post office or on the corner, speak life into someone. Be more alert as you move through the day. Don't miss your assignment for and from God.

> *Let your light so shine before men, that they may see your good works and glorify your Father in heaven.*
>
> MATTHEW 5:16

LET GOD BE GOD

FELISA WARD

"Trust in the Lord with all your heart, and lean not on your own understanding; in all your ways acknowledge Him, and He shall direct your paths." —Proverbs 3:5-6

One Sunday service my spouse, children and I attended Word of Faith Family Worship Center (which was then the old Sam's Club). The spirit of God was extremely high, and I remember Bishop saying we were going to receive testimonies about God's miraculous healing power.

After praise and worship, we prepared for tithes and offerings. As I sat preparing to place my tithes into my envelope, everything went black. I could not see anything, but could hear everything. My first emotion was fear as I began to hyperventilate. Simultaneously, I reached over for my husband's hand and asked him if I was talking to loud? He responded, "No," and proceeded with "What's wrong?" I remember squeezing his hand and telling him that everything was black and dark and I could not see anything. Immediately, after I stated that everything was black and dark, I could not hear anything my husband spoke. As my husband continued to hold my hand I heard in my right ear as the Lord spoke these words, "I am healing you from diabetes," and then instantly I heard a pop sound and my sight was restored.

On the following Monday I scheduled an appointment to see my primary physician. I told him what God had done and said. God instructed me to request a glucose and urinalysis test to see what my glucose levels were. Without any hesitation my primary physician ordered the test and the results confirmed what the Lord spoke. I was in the beginning stage of type II diabetes. As of today, August 30, 2015, my glucose levels have declined and are continuously declining! The Lord is healing me!

My testimony brings to remembrance, Psalms 139:1-4 for we serve an all knowing God! Always remember that what is unseen or unknown by you is always seen and known by our Father.

TILL DEATH DO US PART

DON WILLIAMS

I "Big City", Don Williams met "Small Town Girl", Nakita Barnwell in Fayetteville, North Carolina. We grew up under different circumstances with different beliefs. We came from single parent homes with mothers as the head of the household. The only thing we knew about our fathers was that they chose to abandon their families for various reasons. So the only thing we knew about marriage was what we saw in other relationships and on television. We learned that we are supposed to always be in love, we need to have kids, and as a man, I was supposed to go to work and take care of my family.

According to Proverbs 18:22, "When a man finds a wife he finds a good thing." So, I was very excited to get married, and I knew that it was supposed to be, "till death do us apart." I thought that once we became married we would live happily ever after. That was not the case. We found out quickly that we had a lot to learn. We met in our early 20s and dated for six months before deciding to marry. In the midst of God maturing two childish, self-centered individuals we made lots of mistakes. The three major ones were not keeping God in the forefront of our marriage, me drinking excessively, and Nakita being irresponsible with money as she shopped too much. When we got married Nakita wasn't saved, and I knew that would present some problems. I never imagined how many issues there would be. The problems included in-laws (out-laws), homelessness, no love for each other, and children just to name a few. Oh yeah, I said we didn't love each other. Isn't love the reason you get married? We didn't know much about building a home or making a family.

We were able to fake it through life until our 14th year anniversary when we moved into the real deal stage of our marriage all hell broke loose between us. My wife couldn't stand to be around me, and I didn't like her much either. I tried to get my wife to go church for years but the answer was,

"I'll go when I get my stuff straight." Eventually, my heart's desire came true. She got saved, but she still didn't want me. We separated for about a year, and I went to stay with my sister. God truly had to take center stage in our marriage. I couldn't minister to her when I talked to her on the phone or via mail. I was so miserable I just continued to cry out to God for His help. One night he told me to, "Shut up, and be the man I created you to be." The only chance I had was if God would intervene on my behalf and He did. He visited my wife one night in November, and she called me and told me she wanted to try and make it work again. I know that God was orchestrating the whole thing. Picture us at my sister's house in the dead of winter and being put out on Christmas day in the snow. She had already accepted a job in Atlanta and found a place to stay. So, I packed up a U-Haul and drove from Chicago and arrived in Atlanta the morning of January 1, 2000. After being in Atlanta a few years we were doing great. I found my passion as a college teacher, and my wife became a facilitator at Wells Fargo. Everything seemed to be turning around, and then I was fired and Nakita was diagnosed with breast cancer.

I thought I knew God and Nikita got saved in 1999, so how could this be happening to us? I was shaken beyond belief to the point of fear. Yea, I know that a Christian isn't supposed to have the spirit of fear but I did. I learned how to trust God all over again. This time, He was asking me to let go of the steering wheel and let Him drive. I had a very hard time totally trusting Him even though I had seen Him work for me all my life. I came to the realization that I could lose my wife of 25 years if He didn't do something. This thought drove me to completely trust and lean on Him like never before. That's the only way I made it through. I never truly understood Romans 8:28, "All things work together for the good of those who love God, to those who are the called according to His purpose," until Nakita became sick.

Now 29 years later, I love my wife and understand what life really means. You can and will find us helping married couples in need of Jesus. The best part of this story to me is that it continues.

> *The LORD has appeared of old to me, saying: "Yes, I have loved you with an everlasting love; Therefore with lovingkindness I have drawn you.*
>
> JEREMIAH 31:3

TV FANTASIES ARE NOT LIFE'S REALITY

NAKITA WILLIAMS

"The Cosby Show," "Good Times" and "Married with Children," were shows I watched growing up in my mom's house. It was a single-family home, but I had expectations of being a wife someday. These three TV shows were pretty much all I had to go by as an example of marriage. Not realizing how my child life could impact my future marriage, I felt I was doing pretty well. "The Cosby Show," made me believe I could live a wealthy lifestyle and just smile all the time like Mrs. Huxtable. Or like, "Good Times," I could struggle a lot and be tired every time I came home from work. Like, "Married with Children," I could have children that were very disobedient and a husband that was a slob who drank beer all the time.

Realistically, none of these shows presented what really happens in marriages and what it takes to keep the marriage going. They never showed how to display love to a spouse or how to forgive. They never showed what the pastor said, "For richer or poorer, for better or worse, through sickness and in health." Really, I just said the words and did not realize what I was signing up for. My husband and I tried to find our way, we were homeless and didn't know where our next dinner was coming from. With a child by our side, we often moved from place to place. At that point, I was scared to death. I thought, "Is this what marriage is all about?"

Try having hamburgers for Thanksgiving dinner, or wives try holding down the entire family financially and still having to submit to your husband who was a stay-at-home dad. At times I was angry because I could not buy lipstick or a new dress, but God said I never seen the righteous forsaken or His seed begging for bread. None of those TV shows explained how to be a submissive wife. Slowly but surely God was growing the both of us, strengthening us year after year. Because we did not know God's plan for us, we became weak and vulnerable at times in our marriage. None of the shows told you how to have faith. I don't even believe I saw an episode where any of them went to church unless it was a funeral.

In 2012, while my husband was out of work and near the two-year mark of unemployment, I was diagnosed with breast cancer. My husband would have to tell you what went through his mind. I realized that God had prepared me, for He will never leave me nor forsake me. He kept me through all three surgeries and He kept the laughter between me and my husband even though we did not have a wing to hold on to. Each drive down Highway 75 to 285 to Northside Hospital, not knowing what the doctor would say, could have been the breaking point for us to just give up. I knew I did not want to be like Job's wife and I knew the Word says to walk by faith and not by sight and weeping may endure for a night, but joy comes in the morning. I thought, "When is my morning Lord?"

"Hold on," "Keep the faith," "Your love is growing stronger" and "You will have a great testimony," were all the thoughts that ran through my head. Tough times do not mean give up, they mean that God loves and trusts you to share with the next couple how to get through.

He is no respecter of persons. If He did it for me, He will do it for you. We have gone down in the valley of our marriage and up in the mountain. Twenty-nine years later, the love is easier, the joy is amazing and we are still dating each other. Now that we look back, we know God has been in the mix the entire way.

God got you. Let go and let Him be the role model for your life because TV fantasies are not life's realities.

> *... above all, taking the shield of faith with which you will be able to quench all the fiery darts of the wicked one.*
>
> EPHESIANS 6:16

THE SHEKINAH GLORY OF GOD

NAOMI WILLIAMS

God is so awesome in my life and I don't know what I would do without Him or how I would function on a daily basis. However, my faith has not always been strong and solid. I am the fourth of five children and grew up in the country on a farm. Hard work, immaculate housekeeping, perfect school attendance, good grades, loving your family and community, attending church all day on Sunday, and vacation Bible school during the summer were the norms. I believed what my parents, pastor and Sunday school teacher taught me about God, but had not really experienced Him for myself. I was just religious, a good girl and obedient to my parents.

After graduating high school, my family and I moved to Atlanta so that I could further my education. Being a country girl, I had an acute uneasiness of the big city and trusted way too many people. I was naive to the fact that they were different from the people in the small community I grew up. The noise from trains, buses, emergency vehicles, airplanes, fire trucks, police vehicles, and car horns made it almost impossible to get a peaceful night's sleep or concentrate during the day. It took months to get accustomed after hearing the tranquil sound of crickets, frogs and owls at night in the country. A couple of years later, I accepted Atlanta as home.

I really wanted to be a wife and mother just like my mom. I only wanted a son and a daughter (son first). In June 1963, I birthed a baby boy and I was very happy to be a mom. I said to myself, "All I need now is a little girl and my family will be complete." In July 1964, my daughter was born. It was the proudest moment of my life, so I thought. The morning I was released from the hospital, two doctors and a nurse came into my room and told me that there was a problem with my baby. They said I could go home, but she had to remain. I did not understand because she was so perfect. They informed me that her intestines were twisted and she could not get proper nutrition. When she was ten days old, she underwent surgery to correct the problem. I went to the hospital every day for two months to visit and feed her. I couldn't love on her or hold her the way I desired because she had tubes everywhere. I would just hold her tiny hands and rub her legs and feet. The third month, the doctor said I could bring her home for a one-week trial period, but if she became worse, I had to bring her back immediately. After crying and praying for her healing, she passed at three months old. I lost it. My dream was shattered. I became very depressed and angry. I didn't understand what happened. No matter how much I went to church, prayed, sought answers, it was not helping. One night I prayed until I passed out. I'm not sure how long I was out, but afterward I had such a peace and for the first time, I experienced an enormous manifestation of God's presence and I never questioned my baby's death again.

In August 1965, I birthed the prettiest little baby girl; she was more than I expected – so I thought. After about two months, she started throwing up, losing weight and sleeping too much. I took her to the doctor, but they could not find anything wrong. They changed her formula three different times, but nothing helped. At the time, my son was suffering from asthma and bronchitis. Some days, I would be in the doctor's office with both my babies. At one point, the doctor told me that my son's body was too weak to fight off the infection and he would have to be hospitalized. I said, "No way!" My sister called and said she would keep my baby girl until my son was better. She kept her for about a month but one night she became ill. My sister wanted to take her to the hospital but I said, "No, I will come get her and take her myself." I thought to myself, "Dear God, must I go through this again?" I began praying desperate prayers binding sickness and speaking healing and blessings over my babies; I was not giving up! Needless to say, both my children were miraculously healed by the grace of God. I thank Him every day that they are successful, respectful, responsible and loving adults. They each have two children of their own. My son, who lives in Marietta, has two boys. His oldest is a graduate from University of Georgia and the youngest is a senior at Georgia State University. My daughter, who lives in North Carolina, has a son at Appalachian State University and a daughter in high school.

Fast forward to February 1984. I had another bout with tragedy. My daughter was in college and my son was in the Army. One Saturday morning, my mom fixed breakfast at my sister's house and invited my daughter and me. After we finished breakfast, my mom asked if I would drive her to the drug store to get her medication. She also wanted to talk to me about something. I agreed, and we (my daughter, my niece and my aunt) went on our way to the drug store. We talked, laughed and had a great time. When we arrived to the drug store, my mother and I walked arm in arm to the pharmacy to purchase her medication. The rest of the crew stayed in the car. My aunt wanted an ice cream cone, so I purchased two cones and my mother and I walked back to the car. I handed Mom the ice cream to give to my aunt and when my aunt opened the car door, my mom reached for the door, but fell. I threw my ice cream cone down and ran over to help her, but in my arms she took her last breath. I ran back in the drug store and frantically asked them to call 911. The pharmacist and I ran back to the car and he confirmed what I knew was true, my mom was gone. How could this be when she was laughing and talking a minute ago? It happened so quickly. Again, I was depressed and I questioned myself "What could I have done, how am I going to handle this unspeakable tragedy, why, why, why?" It was very difficult to call my sisters and inform them. We had just left the house and Mom was fine. My two sisters met us at the hospital and we were all in disbelief and very devastated. I thought to myself, "I will never know what my mom wanted to talk to me about." It was very hard for me, I experienced the same Shekinah Glory I experienced during the death of my daughter.

After my mom's funeral, I knew what I had to do. I knew who would help me do it. I totally surrendered my grief to God and wholeheartedly depended on Him. I had to be strong for my daughter who was a college student. This was the first death she grieved of someone very close.

No matter what I go through now or will go through in the future, I know God loves me unconditionally and He can do exceedingly, abundantly, above all that I can ask or think. Even if He doesn't do it the way I would like, I know He is still able. As I always say, not my will God, but Yours be done in my life – and so it is.

> *In this manner, therefore, pray:*
> *Our Father in heaven,*
> *Hallowed be Your name.*
> *Your kingdom come.*
> *Your will be done on earth as it is in heaven.*
> *Give us this day our daily bread.*
> *And forgive us our debts, as we forgive our debtors.*
> *And do not lead us into temptation,*
> *but deliver us from the evil one.*
> *For Yours is the kingdom and the power and the glory forever. Amen.*
>
> MATTHEW 6:9-13

DOWN, BUT NOT OUT!

PAULA WILLIAMS

It felt like a dark and dreary night but… actually, it was a hot summer day when my then husband came into the apartment we lived in with our three small children and took apart the bed he and I shared together. He carried it across the street to the apartment he was now sharing with a woman he met a few months prior. All I remember is my 8-year-old daughter asking, "Dad, what will mom sleep on if you take the bed?" I honestly don't remember his response or if he even responded. I was in such shock and disbelief. I don't even remember what I said, because I was traumatized that my daughter had to witness that scene.

I was married for over 10 years when my husband decided that he did not love me anymore. During those years, we had many struggles, but through them all I never once contemplated a divorce. We were both saved and knew the Lord, so divorce was not an option in my mind. However, he decided that in spite of all that we endured as a couple, the love just wasn't there anymore. I tried convincing him not to allow the enemy to destroy his testimony, but he felt that he had found someone who trusted and believed in him and his dreams, and that was who he wanted to be with.

In our 10 plus years of marriage, we moved fifteen times. My oldest son went to four different elementary schools and we were homeless twice. Motel 6 was one of our stops after the first eviction. But before Motel 6, we had to sleep in our car overnight, because we did not have any money to pay for a room until I received my paycheck the next day. Thankfully, we only had to stay at Motel 6 for one week. The second time we were homeless, I had three children; my youngest was barely a year old. Imagine staying in a homeless shelter with three small children.

Three of the fifteen places we lived in were infested with mice. We would call them, "non-rent paying tenants." Through it all, I never thought about divorce, but I was miserable. You see, he had dreams of having his own business. At first I did not support his dreams of being an entrepreneur. It was mainly because our financial situation was so horrible and our credit was poor. We could not keep our checking account out of the red and we owed utilities in just about every county in metro Atlanta. Each time we moved, we had to make sure it was in a place where we knew we could get the utilities turned on because we always had a balance from previous places we stayed. I just wanted to live a normal life without worrying if something was going to get turned off. Most times we had to pay for things using money orders because our checking accounts would get closed due to poor management. When I tried to get him to budget, his response to me was, "I'm a grown man, and you are not going to tell me what to do with my money!" Getting him to manage money properly was a struggle throughout our marriage. To be honest, I did more fussing than I did praying.

In our ninth year of marriage we were doing much better financially, we even had an active checking account. My husband was working a regular job; however, he still had dreams of being a business owner. This time, I decided to try and support him more and not nag him so much about the finances. I was doing my best to manage the finances. He still did a poor job in this area, so I had to pick up the slack.

At this time, we decided it was time to buy a house, so in my free time on the weekends, while he was working on his business enterprises, I looked at houses. I remember finding two houses, both around $135,000. The next weekend, he went to look at the two houses I found, but then he took me to look at houses worth over $500,000. Clearly, we were not on the same page. To him, my faith was too small. To me, his faith was foolishness! When we needed a new car, he wanted to get a brand new Honda with no money down. We went to several Honda dealerships in the city, and they all turned us down due to our poor credit history. I suggested a Hyundai because at the time they allowed no money down regardless of your credit, but he wanted a Honda with no money. It was a constant battle.

It all came to a head when he left his good-paying job to deal with a situation that came up with the side business he was trying to get off the ground. He literally got fired from his job over the phone on his way to deal with the side business. I was on the other end of the line listening to the entire conversation, I was devastated. By now, I was trying to encourage him in his business dealings but when he got fired, I almost lost it. I tried to be positive, but we did not have any money in savings, so I knew, unless something miraculous happened with his business, we were going to be homeless for a third time.

When he came home from dealing with the issues with his business, he told me he did not love me anymore and that he found someone else who fully supported his business. I could not believe what was happening. We were saved, going to church and serving God throughout all of our struggles, but one thing we failed to do was make prayer a central part of our lives. We never prayed and sought God about our situation; we just went to church – all the time! But we did not allow God to get into the center of our marriage. We did not yield to God as a couple or individually. In the end, my husband decided he found someone else who could be the type of woman he needed.

When my husband and I married, I never lived on my own and I had no real-world experience. I moved from mom's house to living with my husband. So living on my own with three small children was absolutely frightening to me. I did not have a college education, and I had limited skills. I was so afraid, but I did not have time to be fearful long, because I was in Georgia and all of my family lived in Denver. I asked God to help me through this situation (something I should have been doing all along). Through the power of the Lord Jesus, He enabled me to raise my kids and even purchase a home after being divorced from my husband for four years. When my ex-husband attended each of our children's high school graduation all he could say to me was, "You did a wonderful job raising these kids!"

I want to tell you how I survived the last 20 years. After my husband left, I decided not to be a bitter woman. Although most of this story talks about him, I was not perfect. Instead of praying, I was nagging and worrying. But, when he left, I decided that I did not want to be that woman who was always angry at life and at men in particular. I asked the Lord to help me forgive my husband for leaving us the way he did, for bringing his new woman to our child's birthday party while we were still married, for not paying child support, for not taking the initiative to see his children (I mainly had to take them to see him because I needed peace and quiet at times), and for treating me as if he never loved me. I also had to ask God to help me to forgive myself. It's always easy to point the finger at the other person, but it takes two people to make or break a relationship, so I decided to own my part. I had to move on because I had three small children who were depending on me.

Today, I am still single. Yes, it's been twenty years, but I can truly say, I am happy and free. I am complete in Jesus. I desire to be married again, but being whole to me is the most important attribute anyone can have whether single or married. Be complete in Him, first and foremost.

I must say, God truly answers prayers. Believe it or not, I prayed for my ex-husband, his wife and their children. I focused my energy on raising my children and making sure they grew up knowing God and having a well-rounded life as possible. For anyone reading my story that may be experiencing something similar, here is some advice I would like to leave with you:

- Don't keep your children from the other parent.
- Don't bash the other parent in front of your children, let the children form their own opinions.
- Your children are young for a short time; try to focus on their needs because they may be suffering more than you know. Don't ignore your needs, but understand the importance of their needs.
- Seek solace when possible to keep from letting the stress of being a single parent overwhelm you.
- Choose not to be bitter (this is a process, it will not happen overnight).
- Cry hard, but don't cry long.
- Get up and move on, life does not end just because your relationship did.
- Acknowledge your part in the demise of your relationship. It's always easy to point the finger, but when you do that, three more are pointing back at you.
- Sometimes you will be angry; deal with it, but not in front of your children.
- Whatever passion or hobby that you have, keep it, but don't let it become primary to raising your children, and don't make your children your whole world either – they grow up and fast!
- If your spouse remarries or is in another relationship, ask God to strengthen you to interact respectfully with the other person. It is important that you do this to keep your children from having even more stress. It's bad enough for your children to deal with their parents being divorced, but to add fighting parents on top of that is not a good combination for children to witness.
- And the most important thing you can do is pray and when you get tired of praying, pray some more. Allow God to heal you totally and completely. This process may take time, so dating should not be a priority – complete healing should be!

SHOW ME YOU!

NATARSHA J. WILSON

Natarsha J. Wilson
"Grateful"

As my foot touched the last step before arriving onto the patio rooftop, a loud voice from within yelled throughout my body: *"Show Me You!" Show Me You!"* At first I didn't understand the screaming within my spirit. Within the context of the next half hour as the screams continued I better understood.

Let me paint the complete picture. It's a perfect Friday night and I'm on the rooftop with a childhood friend. It was about 10:15 pm. The sky is an awesome pitch black backdrop on a crisp summer night. Stars are twinkling bright as planes cascade thru the sky in-route to and from Hartsfield-Jackson International Airport. The wine is smooth and the conversation upbeat. Life is good, the laughter rich and the voice kept yelling: *"Show Me You!"*

I begin to search the sky for what I could only imagine was about to happen. I had been walking in faith for quite some time. Every day was a victory that I had made it through. But this was about to be different. Mind you, the inner voice continued to scream and I have not uttered a word of this internal battle to my friend as we enjoyed our evening chat.

As I examined the sky, now looking for Him; I understood and braced myself. The human me imagined that He would appear in a cloud formation or outline. I looked among the stars and the clean black backdrop of the night. *Show me you*.....had actually been my spirit calling out; without any assistance from me, to something or someone far greater. But why it was so intense on this day remains His mystery.

Out of no where an awesome rainbow appeared. I jumped to my feet in adulation and respect and threw up my hands in praise while at the same time telling my friend to look. We both were in awe because it's not often that you see rainbows during the night. At that moment I began to also tell my friend how my spirit had been calling out on its own in such a thunderous way and how the sequence played it's self out.

We both ran around the rooftop doing the Happy Dance (like in black churches) and praised God for His awesome ability to show up in our lives no matter the situation. After a few minutes of praising and glorifying, we returned to more discussions, wine and laughter. In a calm manner God revealed himself in the beautiful rainbow. He calmly faded back into the black backdrop of the night. We were forever changed.

I shared my testimony on Monday with a co-worker. Her Aunt, in the same city, had already shared her story with her about seeing a beautiful rainbow in the middle of the night. Another sharing brought even another confirmation from a friend who was walking with her granddaughter outside to empty trash in Charlotte, North Carolina when her granddaughter told her to, *"Look at the rainbow Granny! How is that, It's Night?"*

Show me you was not just about me on that beautiful night but for all spirits open for a sign. On that night, universal God gave global clarity. God will show up in so many different ways, during the most interesting of scenarios. But you must be open and available.

Since that incredible night I have faced various tests on my journey; the diagnosis of Breast Cancer in 2008 being the greatest thus far. When I speak to many a Sur-Thrivors, I have found that my journey was grossly understated by what they had to endure. But what I know for sure is that in the darkness of my journey I served as a light to many that wanted to *"Give Up" because* chemotherapy is not easy.

Expect and seek your touch from God daily. What I know now without a doubt is that at the end of every test, trial and heartache, God will present a rainbow filled with love!

I set my rainbow in the cloud and it shall be for the covenant between Me and the earth.

GENESIS 9:13

SEGREGATION IN MY LIFE: GOD'S DIRECTED PATH

G. PATRICIA WOODWARD

I grew up in the 50s and 60s outside of Baltimore City in a community that was totally segregated. I was the middle child of seven siblings. Our community had the amenities we needed: schools, grocery and drug stores, barber and beauty shops, churches, funeral homes and recreational facilities. The residents ranged from professionals to regular working folks. Families knew each other very well. As children, the neighbors would correct us, just like our parents, when they saw us doing something wrong. Many of our teachers lived in our community and knew our parents which didn't help if you misbehaved in class. Our doctors actually made house calls when needed. The impact of living in this closed-knit community was very positive and nurturing. I received an excellent education, and I have lifelong friends as a result of my childhood environment.

However, segregation had a negative impact on me because I thought, "It just wasn't fair or right." As I studied American History in school, my thought was, "This wasn't what the Preamble to the Constitution stated." It states that, "all men were created equal with certain unalienable rights," but this was not the case for Blacks in America. Even the Emancipation Proclamation didn't correct the injustices Blacks faced in life. As a teenager ready to venture out into the world, this was very disturbing.

I want to share with you a few events and how I responded to living in a segregated society and the impact my actions had on my life. Come journey with me to the 60s.

In 1963, three of my best friends and I decided to venture out and eat at a Chinese restaurant. We entered the restaurant and were met by the owner who was Chinese. Initially, we couldn't understand what he was saying because of his accent and broken English. After he repeatedly made his statements, it finally dawned on us that he was saying we couldn't be served in the restaurant. He was waving his hands and pointing to the back of the restaurant. He meant for us to go to the outside in the back, and he would take our orders. Needless to say, we didn't have Chinese food that night. Our shared thoughts were, "How can he deny us service, be prejudice, and have a business when he probably wasn't even born here and could hardly speak English?" We were born in the United States, but denied our rights to be served by a foreigner. This incident didn't sit well with me at all.

So, shortly after that I became a civil rights activist by joining the Congress for Racial Equality (CORE) and from that point my marching and picketing days had begun. The National Director for CORE was James Farmer.

Each Saturday, my friends and I marched on a segregated skating rink in suburban Baltimore with other members of CORE. The owner refused to allow Blacks in the rink and was quite passionate about his position. Each Saturday, the leaders and participants of the picket would get on a bus and go to the area of the skating rink. We then would meet in the basement of a Black church to plan our strategy. Plans would be made to determine how many people would break the picket line, stand at the entrance of the skating rink and refuse to move when ordered by the police. Of course, because they refused to move, they would be arrested. The number of picketers that would be arrested was based on how much money was in the treasury of that particular chapter of CORE. These picketers had to be bailed out of jail. Eventually, because of the picketing, which resulted in a loss of business as well as the owner's refusal to integrate, the business closed.

I participated in the March on Washington on August 28, 1963. That is one day I will never forget. I remember very well how the expressway from Baltimore to Washington was absolutely bumper-to-bumper with cars, trucks, and buses making their way to the, "March." Riders in other cars were waving, smiling and singing as we passed each other on the expressway. It was a very humid day but thousands of people, estimated at about 250,000, were there for a purpose. The purpose was to let America know, "Racial injustices must end!" Martin Luther King's, "I Have a Dream," speech made history and called for the unity of all regardless of race, religion, age, sex, or financial status. This, "March" impacted the whole nation and world. President Lyndon B. Johnson signed into law after Congress passed the Civil Rights Act of 1964. The Voting Rights Act was passed shortly afterwards in 1965.

Another march I participated in was at the World's Fair in 1994 in New York. I couldn't believe it – there were certain pavilions that didn't allow Blacks to come in to view the exhibits. How could this be? This was the World's Fair and it was in New York. New York where the Statue of Liberty stands boldly and declares, "Give me your tired, your poor, your huddled masses yearning to breathe free." It rained most of the day, but we marched and sang in our picket lines with our signs.

I graduated from high school in June 1965 and then attended Howard University in Washington, D.C. I had the opportunity to see and hear from activists such as Stokely Carmichael, H. Rap Brown and Dick Gregory. These experiences made me more sensitive to any form of injustices. To this day, I still get emotional when I hear the songs, "We Shall Overcome," "Ain't Going to Let Nobody Turn Me Around" and especially Martin Luther King's "I Have a Dream" Speech. It brings back the memories of my days participating in the Civil Rights movement with CORE.

In my life now, I try to share my stories of life struggles in the 60s with people I meet, especially young people. I try to impress upon them that even with the injustices we faced, we didn't give up because we had faith in God. I also emphasize to them that many people marched, suffered, fought and died so that the inequalities we endured wouldn't continue in the United States. The rights and privileges we have today are a result of their dedication to that purpose. I remind them to exercise these rights and not abuse them. Also, I share how faith in God kept us uplifted and strong. We are all God's creation and we must live according to His righteousness.

I couldn't understand why one human being would treat another one badly just because of the color of their skin, but I have grown in the knowledge of my Lord and Savior and I understand that He is in control. One of my favorite scriptures that has helped me in so many situations is Proverbs 3:5-6. It states, "Trust in the Lord with all thine heart; and lean not unto thine own understanding. In all thy ways acknowledge him and he shall direct thy path." So, I've trusted God!

> *It's the action, not the fruit of the action, that's important. You have to do the right thing. It may not be in your power, may not be in your time, that there'll be any fruit. But that doesn't mean you stop doing the right thing. You may never know what results come from your action. But if you do nothing, there will be no result.*
>
> MAHATMA GANDHI

DO NOT JUDGE A BOOK BY ITS COVER

BERNICE WRIGHT

Bernice G. Wright

At the age of 17, I met the man of my dreams on an unexpected blind date. Meeting this man truly helped me learn not to judge a book by its cover. One day my twin sister's boyfriend arrived to our house unannounced with a friend. Little did I know, they had plans for a double date. My twin answered the door and came to let me know about their plans; I was shocked! I had never seen nor heard of this man and had no interest in dating at that time. We later found out that my sister's boyfriend had shown his friend a picture of my twin and said, "There is another one just like her, do you want to meet her?" That is how they ended up on our doorstep that day.

Now when my twin came to me she said he was very good looking. Knowing the prankster that she was I needed to see for him myself. I quietly peeked around the corner and saw Mr. Harold L. Wright, a tall handsome man in an Air force uniform. Holy cow! Suddenly, I was ready for a date. We went to the drive-in theater and had a great time. The only flaw I found in this handsome man was that he talked so slowly that my twin and I spent the whole night secretly laughing at him.

On the way home a reckless driver nearly caused us to have a terrible accident. By the grace of God, Harold's quick thinking and great driving skills saved our lives that night. I was so grateful for that slow-talking man who not only saved me that night but changed my life forever. Within a year we were married and spent 52 years together until 2010 when the Lord called my beloved husband home.

What is marriage? Marriage is a commitment; it is not just about looks or lust of the flesh. Marriage is a vow made between two people, "Until life and death do we part." It is not what your mate can do for you but what can be accomplished together as one producing seed and being a light for future generations. A wife of noble character is her husband's crown, but a disgraceful wife is like decay in his bones (Proverbs 12:4).

Over those 52 years, despite many ups and downs, we were never separated. I know without a shadow of doubt that, it was God who put us together and kept us together. Study Ephesians 5:21-33 as you submit to one another in the fear of God.

> *What greater thing is there*
> *for two human souls,*
> *than to feel that they are joined*
> *for life-to strengthen each other in all labor,*
> *to rest on each other in all sorrow,*
> *to minister to each other in silent unspeakable*
> *memories at the moment of the last parting?*
>
> GEORGE ELIOT

MAMA ALWAYS CAME THROUGH

JACKIE D. YOUNG

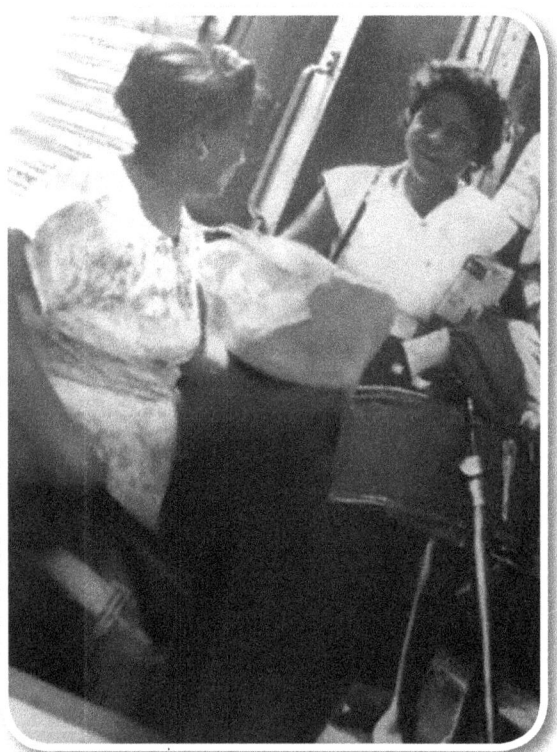

When I look back over my life, there are two significant circumstances that let me know that the Holy Spirit was working in my life. I was not only unaware of His presence, but I didn't even know anything about Him. The two significant circumstances involved my mother and her ability, with the help of God, to be there when I needed her.

The first situation occurred when I was 8 years old. My sister and I were living in Jacksonville, Florida, with our dad. I was unhappy with this arrangement, so I devised a secret plan that would get us back with our mom who moved to West Palm Beach from Lake City, Florida, during the spring of third grade. She left my sister and me in the care of her close friend, so that we wouldn't have to change schools near the end of the term.

When my dad learned about this, he came and took us to Jacksonville as soon as the school year ended before my mom could come for us. This was very traumatic for me, because I knew my mother did not know about this. By the end of the summer, my sister and I decided that we would rather stay in Jacksonville for the next school year. We had made many friends over the summer versus West Palm Beach where we didn't know anyone. We were living with my dad's girlfriend, and after a while seemed more like we were living with Cinderella's stepmother. Our dad was not around very much so he didn't know how we were being treated. There was no physical abuse, but I felt like a servant who had no privileges and was constantly under the watchful eye of a master. All correspondence to and from our mother was read by the girlfriend and she listened in on all phone calls. I knew that I had to find a way to let my mother know what was going on. How could I do this? Finally I got an idea!

I would secretly go to the post office and mail a letter to my mother on one of my errands to the supermarket. The post office was just a couple of blocks further than the supermarket. Somehow, I managed to get my hands on enough change for a stamped envelope (approximately 10 cents) and kept it hidden. Once I had the money to mail my letter, I waited for the next time I was sent to the supermarket. When the time came, I hid a piece of paper in my shoe. I knew there were pens at the post office. I was always timed when I went anywhere, so to make up for the extra time I needed, I ran to the post office and quickly wrote one line to my mom, "Mama, come see about us."

The following Saturday my mother arrived. When she went to the bathroom, I followed and sat on the side of the tub and told her everything that had been going on. That Monday, she withdrew us from school and took us back to West Palm Beach with her where I remained under her loving care until I graduated from high school. When I went off to college, the following events began to unfold.

When I was 19 years old, I made a very important decision without praying to God or even consulting an adult. This story tells about my experience of realizing the dilemma I was in, turning to God in faith and how He came through for me.

On January 29, 1963, I eloped with my first husband. We were engaged to be married but had not yet determined a date. At that time, I was a sophomore at Howard University in Washington, D.C. During semester break I traveled to Brooklyn where my fiancé was employed and we decided to get secretly married and still have a wedding later without revealing that we were already married. Well, it seemed that we had a good plan since our families were in Florida and would not be aware of our relationship. What we didn't plan on was my getting pregnant when I, unbeknownst to our families, went to spend my spring break with him.

What in the world had I done? Now I realized that I didn't want to be married not to mention have a baby. I greatly feared my mom's reaction to this news. My college roommate and I developed an elaborate scheme with the cooperation of his mother to keep the news from my mom until after the baby was born in January. However, when she learned that I had left the campus for two weeks between the spring and summer terms, it was necessary for me to share the news with her to explain my absence from school.

Although disappointed, she was determined to do all she could to see that I completed my college education even agreeing to keep the baby until after my graduation. I transferred to Long Island University for my junior year to be with my husband until the baby was born. He promised my mother that he would see to it that I completed my degree. As the deadline for registration grew near, I realized that he had no intention of providing me with the money I needed to register. On the last day of registration, I went to the campus to register without a dime to pay the required fees. I went through the registration process and when told by the cashier the amount I owed, I informed her that I did not have any money. After having to repeat this to her several times, she directed me back to the registrar's office. I repeated the same information to the lady at the desk explaining to her that because this was the last day to register, I had to come even though I did not have any money. She agreed to keep my class cards on her desk until 2:00 the next day. My registration would be canceled if I had not returned with the money.

I informed my mother-in-law of my situation. She told me that she was not able to help me (she owned 16 apartments). I asked that she speak with my mother since my mother did not have a telephone at her house. My mother was a beautician who barely made enough money to pay her bills. When I spoke back with my mother-in-law later that night, as I already knew, my mother did not have the money I needed. At first, I was discouraged and began to cry as I walked back to my apartment from the telephone booth. Suddenly, I stopped, wiped my tears, and said to the Lord, "Lord, I know that I have you in my corner and as long as I have you in my corner, I might be delayed but I will NEVER be defeated. If you want me to go to school, the money will come. If it does not come, then I will know that it's Your will that I not go at this time."

I went home, went to bed and slept soundly. The next day, once 2:00 came and no money, I was resolved to the fact that I would not be going to school. Around 3:00 there was a knock on the door. It was a fellow from Western Union with a money order for me. I said to myself, "It is too late." Then the thought came (Now I know it was the Holy Spirit) to go to the school anyway. I hurried because the office closed at 4:00. When I reported to the lady who was holding my cards, she said she was expecting me. She said that my mother had called and told her not to cancel my registration because the money was on the way. The importance of her statement is that I never spoke directly to my mother regarding the situation. She and I had not really discussed my enrollment at this school in any detail, since it occurred after I married and moved to New York.

My mother had no names or direct numbers. How was she able to speak directly with the person who was holding my registration? *Mama always came through.*

---

*All that I am,
or hope to be,
I owe to my angel mother.*

ABRAHAM LINCOLN

A Message from Paula Palmer Green
The Legacy Book Visionary & Project Manager

In order to move forward, sometimes you have to look back. Sometimes you have to reflect and bring to remembrance the people in your life who showed you unconditional love. It is love that gives us what we need to live a life that reflects why God sent His only begotten Son into the world.

After all is said and done, a person's legacy is merely how deeply they express their love to humankind. As Christians, we are taught about love in its infinite form by studying the life of our Savior – Jesus Christ. The more we submit ourselves to God's will for our life, the more impact we will have on the lives of others.

These stories serve as a reminder that each and every day you are given a second chance to love deeper. You will also be reminded to trust God when you cannot see Him or when He doesn't answer immediately. You will be inspired to treat people kinder and forgive those who you don't think deserves to be forgiven. Each and every day God gives you grace to help others get to know Him by telling what He has done for you.

You have been given gifts, talents and life to build His kingdom by sharing your story. There is something special about you that someone is waiting to experience. It is my prayer that after reading this book, you will be inspired to take God at His Word. And apply His Word to your living as you become the person He made you to be and live the life you imagine!

May the blessings of your legacy
live beyond your appointed days.

Acknowledgements

Marian Barnes
Sandra Bethea
Pastor Christopher Boyd
Bishop Dale C. Bronner
Dr. Nina Bronner
Gerren Clark
Ashley Davidson
Mercedes Douglas
Billie Green
Linda D. Green
Yolanda Harris
Gilbert Hunter
Anita Minniefield
Danica Peoples
Mallorie Pirita
Bonnie Trice
Paula Williams
Rev. Courtney Wright
Word of Faith Family Worship Cathedral's Leaders, Staff, Family & Friends

"The greatest legacy one can pass on to one's children and grandchildren is not money or other material things accumulated in one's life, but rather a legacy of character and faith."

BILLY GRAHAM

To order more copies or schedule a consultation to publish
a book for your organization, visit:

www.SeasonedSaintsLegacyBook.org
or
call 404.907.0530